# A Back~
## ~Fence Story

*drawings by* DAVID

STONE MARTIN

# A Back~ ~Fence Story

by *Augusta Walker*

New York / 1967

ALFRED · A · KNOPF

*This is a Borzoi Book*

*Published by* ALFRED A. KNOPF, INC.

*Published February 20, 1967*
*Second Printing, March 1967*

© *Copyright 1966 by Augusta Walker*

*All rights reserved under International and Pan-American Copyright*
*Conventions.*

*Distributed by Random House, Inc. Published simultaneously in*
*Toronto, Canada, by Random House of Canada Limited.*

*Library of Congress Catalog Card Number: 66-21363*

*Manufactured in the United States of America*

# Contents

# A Back~
## ~Fence Story

## Chapter 1

# Where They Came From in the First Place

It is not easy to say where cats came from in the first place. For our purposes here it all started with a little gray-striped cat walking along the fence looking for a place to live, but of course that only brings up the question where she was before and why she came from there. One is tempted to say simply that cats were here from the beginning like most things, but that stirs up many other questions, such as how it all happened and whether anything really had a beginning. So perhaps we should confine ourselves to the assumption that where civilization produces back yards and board fences, nature produces cats. These things occur together. And so by natural process a little gray cat with green eyes found itself walking along a fence looking for a place to live, and we can judge from what happened afterwards something of what had happened before.

She had certainly had a home once, for she proved later to know all about stoves and refrigerators. She knew about people too. She tried to judge from their looks whether it would be worth while to approach them and rub against their legs, purring. And when, in her tour of this particular block of yards and fences, she passed along by a little garden in which somebody with approachable looks was sitting in a blue canvas chair reading a book, and through an open back door she glimpsed a white stove and refrigerator in a red kitchen, she felt at once that this was her kind of place. Not that she was obvious about it. She passed right on by without pausing, but a little farther on, she turned and came back for another look. That garden had three ailanthus trees in it, two to-together in the middle and one at the side, and there were green plants growing underneath. There was also a cement space, and there were four windows, all open, two of them with curtains and flowerpots, and a cellar pit below, and the other two, on the jutting-out side which was the kitchen, crossed by iron bars which a cat could just slip through nicely. And an open door. Everything was most convenient for cats.

Meanwhile she had found other places to eat. She knew her way up and down a jagged wall at the end of the block, and at the bottom were some garbage cans beside which somebody left scraps of food every morning on a piece of paper. She also knew some front steps near the street where food was left. But she kept coming back every day to have a better look at this place. Usually the door and windows were all open and the same person was sitting in the canvas chair with books and papers around. This person always noticed the little gray cat strolling by, but evidently did not yet suspect that it was making up its mind to live here. The cat was in no hurry, for the weather was fine and she was comfortable.

What she needed a home for was to have her family in. She was already expecting this family, but it was still a long way off and didn't show on her at all yet. Besides, she was content to roam around through the drowsy end-of-summer days. A few leaves were falling, and the sun shone through the bare places in the trees, making pleasant, warm spots below where she could curl up and nap. She felt leisurely and at ease. She tried napping once in a while in this yard, and the person in the chair did not mind.

Her old home had probably been a good one, but it was so completely lost that she had given up trying to find it. It was the sort of accident that often happens to a young cat. No doubt at a certain time she noticed that she was beginning to have male callers outside her window, and she wanted so badly to get acquainted with them that, although she was tightly shut in, she found a way out. And since she had never been out before, she could not find her way home again.

At first she didn't care. She was so interested in her new companions that even eating seemed unimportant, and for several days they had a gay time together, romping and dallying around. But a day came, and quite soon, when they all grew tired of it, and one by one the male cats departed for their old haunts. The little gray cat was abandoned and homeless. Fortunately she was not the worrying kind.

Still, it took her a long time to move into that house she had selected. The person in possession, whose name turned out to be Ann, did not mind a cat in her yard, but when it tried to come inside, she said, "Shoo!" and "Scat!" and made it plain that *no cats were wanted there*. Those were her days of resistance. The little gray cat (whose name had been lost along with her old home) kept on trying to move in, but for weeks she made no progress at all. As soon as she came in the door, she was pushed out a window, and as soon as she came in a window she was pushed out the door. But she never lost heart. Sometimes she managed to curl up in a corner somewhere and catch a quick nap before she was found and thrown out. What difference did it make whether she napped in the yard or in the house? And whether she was there ten minutes or an hour? She wasn't causing any trouble, and she could eat somewhere else until this person relented. The place suited her perfectly. There were couches and chairs around the big room and plenty of openings for entrance and exit. And there were nice nooks between chests and bookshelves where kittens might be comfortably born and safely kept. Why should anybody object to a few kittens in a corner? New kittens couldn't hurt a thing, and they would make no work for anybody except herself. This Ann seemed to have nothing very important to do that would interfere with the normal life of a cat and her family. Most of the time she was just sitting outside with a mess of papers around. Or she was in the kitchen cooking and eating something or in the big room pushing a dust mop around the floor. Sometimes she went away and was gone for several hours, but she al-

ways left a kitchen window open, and then the cat slipped in through the bars and stayed for a long time without Ann ever knowing it. So what harm could there be in staying all the time?

Now the weather was growing colder and it was often gloomy. There were strong winds and sometimes a cold sleety rain that made the fallen leaves on the ground dank and soggy. All this time the cat was swelling bigger around the middle, and at last she began to worry. Windows and doors were shut everywhere. What would she do with a family of new kittens in a cold rain? In the days when she romped with the boy cats she had not known about the winter.

One drizzly night Ann went away and stayed late. The little cat found the window open a few inches at the bottom and squeezed through. Inside the big room she saw a door standing ajar, and she went snooping through it back into a closet. In the farthest corner she discovered a box with some shoes in it. She pushed and pulled the shoes around in the box until she could lie down on them without discomfort. This, she decided, was the place to have her kittens when the time arrived. Ann came home late that night, and when she put her clothes in the closet, she found that box of shoes occupied by a cat. What can you do with a pregnant cat on a cold, wet night? There is nothing to do. The cat stayed where it was. The next day Ann took the shoes out of the box, put a piece of blanket in it, and moved it to a better place between some bookshelves and a chest of drawers, where it was protected and darkened behind the kitchen door standing open. It was just the kind of place that kittens would choose for themselves to be born in if they could.

Never was a cat so happy as this one when Ann put her into the box to show that it was hers, and afterwards gave her some scraps of chicken and some milk. The cat kept going back to her corner to try out her box and knead the blanket softly with her paws. A few nights later, when again rain was dripping outside, four kittens were born into that box, and they were very relieved to find themselves in a comfortable nook.

This is where they came from in the first place, as far as can be determined. Of course it all goes back much farther than that, but it seems necessary to begin in the middle of things and proceed from there, much as we would like to know how all things began. The little gray cat is not a main character in our story, but at least two of the main characters have now made their entrance: the two little black sisters, Bug and Nosey. Later on Ann took the little gray-striped brothers somewhere else to live. And to tell the truth, their mother went somewhere else to live too. For, although she adored those kittens and took care of them like the most doting of mothers, when they were big enough to eat their food from a saucer, the time came for her to go back to the fence and the male cats again, for she was a little tramp at heart, and they lured her away to some new territory, where (we can guess) she went through the whole process all over, and we hope found some new person to fix her a box in a corner.

But Bug and Nosey stayed with Ann, and they grew up happily together.

# Chapter 2
# *A Nice Tight Universe*

Bug and Nosey looked alike except for their faces. They were both black with white feet and breasts and a little peninsula of white underneath their chins to the tip. The difference was that on Nosey's chin the white was lopsided—it spilled over onto the right side of her nose and made a funny little white spot there. This was why she was called Nosey. But the name suited her in other ways too, for, as she grew up, she loved to sniff into other people's houses and affairs. Bug achieved her name by becoming, very young, a relentless bug catcher, waiting for hours under the kitchen sink for one to come out. Her markings were perfectly balanced and neat, and the slender white peninsula on her chin exquisitely drawn. When she sat with her head lifted, looking up, showing her white throat and chin, she was a lovely sight. It was as if she had been marked by some fastidious artist who would do only perfect work, but when Nosey's turn came, she jerked and the white was spilled. But they both became beautiful cats. Their fur grew blacker and very lustrous and plushy as they grew older.

Their personalities were quite different. From the beginning Nosey was a little silly, but Bug was a thoughtful type. Nosey would begin meowing and forget what she was meowing about. She liked a great deal of attention and would climb all around Ann's neck and shoulders so as not to be forgotten. But Bug was more self-sufficient. The deep, strong life inside her could be seen in her eyes. When the pupils were expanded wide and perfectly round like bottomless, glistening black pools, with only a thin green encircling rim, the mystery lurking in their depths could be seen, but not what made the mystery or where it came from. Even as a tiny kitten she had that secret depth. When she sat very still with her neat little white-tipped paws in front of her and those black pools quite round, she seemed to be wondering about her own mystery and feeling it inside her as if it had pushed her into being through its force, and she questioned what it wanted of her. Whatever it is that nature in her hidden plans wants cats to do, Bug was ready for it, for she had all the winning softness and muscular fierceness that are needed in this world: the soft little padded feet with their sharp claws, the delicate and graceful form that could slither and sloop along, making all corners into curves, or spring several feet straight up in the air without even jumping.

Throughout their kittenhood Bug and Nosey were the closest of friends. They romped wildly together, racing round and over the furniture and up and down the drapes. They would go into a tight clinch, biting, hissing, and spitting, and roll over and over. And finally, worn out, they would fall exhausted on a couch in a close hug and lick each other's faces until they fell asleep. They never slept apart, and so they never knew a moment's loneliness, though Ann often went away and stayed for hours. They preferred to have her there, but they always had each other. They could sleep, wake up, play, fight, and sleep some more until she came back and it was time to eat again.

Meanwhile it was winter, and they had never yet been outside. They did not realize that there was an outside, although they could climb up on the window sills and see out. They found it very interesting to sit there and look at the yard, trees, fences, and buildings, and wonder what it must be like out there. But they did not know for sure whether all that was real. It looked real, and some things moved, but they always bumped their noses against the glass that formed the wall of their world. Perhaps those trees and buildings and board fences were not really there, but it made little difference, since the world they were in was big enough, and they never expected to need more. There was plenty of space to explore and race around in and there were lots of obstacles to plunge up and over. In fact, they hoped that this was the whole of creation and that nobody would ever live in it except themselves and Ann, since two kittens are enough for each other, and one person is enough to take care of them. A world seems safer if you are familiar with all its corners early in your life and if the same cats and people are always there so that you know them very well and can tell what to expect of them. Then if one or two strange people come in now and then from outer space, it does not matter. They usually prove to be harmless and can safely be climbed around on. After a while they go away again, leaving the same arrangement as before.

But one day something happened that made their lives altogether different and never again quite so safe as they had thought. The sun was shining brightly through the windows, and suddenly Ann opened a door at the end of the kitchen where they had never known there was a door. A rush of cold, sunny air came in. No glass was there to hinder them from stepping straight out beyond the known boundaries. The kitchen floor simply came to an end at a little ledge that they could jump off, and after they had nosed around very carefully for a few minutes, they tried it, Bug first. There they were on a stretch of cement in bright sunlight with no roof above them. It was astonishing. As soon as they had jumped off the ledge, they changed their minds and jumped back on it, Nosey first. Then they peeped around and thought about it for a while. Just then Ann stepped over their heads, walked right out, bent over, and began to dig. She called to them, and they soon gathered up their courage to jump off the step again. The first thing they wondered was how big this space might be, or whether it was just indefinite. Kittens feel nervous about anything indefinite. They would prefer it to have sides and corners that are always where you can find them, like the little box they were born into, which seemed so big to them at the time, and later the room, which was much the same on a bigger scale and seemed specially made for the expansion of their needs. So they hoped to find that this too was a box. With Bug leading the way they began to make expeditions across the cement. Where it came to an end there was soft, crumbly ground, and a little distance from here were two big rough tree trunks together that went high up and branched out on all sides.

Meanwhile Ann was walking around doing amazing things. She was carrying buckets and tools, digging holes in the soft ground, and pouring water in them. Next she was sweeping up the cement with a broom. They found all this exciting. The bright sun was pleasant and the air was livelier out here. It felt cold and warm at the same time, and it made them energetic. They scampered back and forth and climbed a little way up the tree trunks. This was an outlet for them, a place to be more free in. They ran around Ann and clambered on her back as she stooped over. The soft dirt that came out of the holes she was digging seemed wonderful stuff. They dug some little holes of their own in it, and Bug had the idea that they might come here sometimes instead of going to their sandbox inside. It even occurred to her to try it now, but Nosey pounced on her and interrupted. So she put it off for the time being.

Before long the sun disappeared behind a building. They all went inside and the door was closed. But now they knew about the other world, and after that they went out there often. Soon a very warm day came, so warm that the door was left open all day long, and they could go in and out as they pleased. It seemed thrilling to have so much liberty. By now they had found all the four corners of the garden and were satisfied. It too was a box and just the right size. The three board walls reached up high enough to shut out whatever was beyond, so that it could never come in. Kittens like a nice tight universe with good walls to it, and they would rather not know what is outside—for if there is anything there, it must be dreadful.

Still, you couldn't be sure about what might be already in, at least when the sun was gone and the dusk falling. Night was exciting and dangerous. Now that the weather was warm, Ann left the door open at night too, but she closed an ironwork door which seemed especially good for keeping big things out but not keeping little things in. Bug and Nosey could creep underneath or go through any of the spaces in the grillwork. They were a little jumpy about the whole thing, and their large eyes full of expectation. Nosey was jumpier than Bug; she preferred to be inside close to Ann's feet while Ann was getting supper ready. Bug couldn't resist scaring her a few times by plunging in fiercely, pretending that she was some terrible monster from beyond the outer walls. This was such fun because Nosey believed it every time. Her back shot up into a tight bend, her tail bushed out, and she spat like a small explosion. It filled Bug with glee to see Nosey go into a fit like that. It became a game, but they always lost their heads and thought it was real. They had never known any danger, but in their little cat souls they understood all about it and were just practicing for the day when it would come.

## Chapter 3

# The Outside Gets Bigger

Now that they knew the garden, they began to make other discoveries. There were some long cracks in the board wall on one side, and through these they could see scriggles and bits and slices of something. It looked, in fact, as though there might be a place over there not unlike the place they were in. They could glimpse cement and some green stems near the cracks. Every time they ran around the yard they passed those cracks, and often they stopped to see if what they thought was there before was still there. But the cracks were narrow, and nothing that could be seen through them had any kind of wholeness about it. There were just slivers, and a sliver doesn't give you much of an idea as to what a complete object is like above and below the sliver. And now when Bug and Nosey climbed high on the tree trunks, they noticed that beyond the board walls there were bushes which must be rooted down below. In short, they began to suspect that there was somewhere else to go, and soon after, they began to want to go there.

They were big kittens now, and climbing was easy enough. All they needed was some kind of goal to climb toward. A board fence should have a top and another side, and the normal kitten will quickly find this out and start an investigation to determine just where and what are the boundaries of its proper roaming area, although some peril will be encountered.

Bug was first. She climbed up a corner of the fence a few times and saw that there were pickets along the top, but Ann always came and took her off before she had a chance to slip between them. Of course there was not the least sense in Ann's trying to keep her from going over the fence. Cats and board fences go so naturally together that one would seem unfulfilled without the other, and it is futile to try to thwart their relationship. Not that Ann was really trying to do such a thing. She understood the nature of cats and fences. She simply thought that Bug and Nosey were still too young. People like Ann always think that. It is up to the cat itself to know, and fortunately Bug did. She never gave up the idea, although she was picked off the fence many times. But Ann could not always be watching. So at last Bug made it over the top and went sliding and tumbling down the other side, landing on some soft earth among those twisting stems, which turned out to be quite big shrubs.

Bug knew that now she was off her own property and on somebody else's. She knew that anything might happen, that Ann could not rescue her. She was taking great risks. She stayed quietly in the bushes for a few minutes, with her heart beating fast, hoping that nothing would happen, and as nothing did, she crept out onto the cement and nosed around the corners of some wooden boxes. She drew herself up on one of them to see what was in it. There was more earth inside and some plants. Further on she found a lot of green ivy vines and an iron chair frame like Ann's.

Still nothing was happening, but Bug decided she had done enough for one day. The important test was whether she could get back without trouble. She made her way to the corner, clambered upwards to the top, and sat there a moment to look around, feeling the exhilaration of success. Then her heart gave a big thump. Only a few feet from here, lying on top of the adjoining fence, was a large, clean white cat sleepily sunning itself and looking at her with no particular expression in its yellowish eyes. Bug had never been face to face with a strange cat before—only now and then she had seen one from the window—and she did not know whether a strange cat was naturally friendly or not. She remembered only her mother, that creature who had nursed her, washed her, kept her warm, and protected her from everything; and with the shy hope that perhaps all grown-up cats were a little like that, she approached this one a few steps. It looked at her, sleepy and indifferent. In the bright sun the pupils of its eyes were almost invisible. Bug went another step or two, and suddenly the white cat opened its red mouth wide and hissed. For an instant Bug was stunned. Her back went up automatically, and in two seconds she was down off the fence and in the house, back in the farthest corner under the bed, where she stayed until Ann came in the other door with a bag full of groceries.

It was several days before Bug had the courage to do any more exploring, but meanwhile Nosey, who did not know about the white cat, was trying a few things. She had climbed one of the trees to the first limb and found that if you eased yourself out along it, clinging tightly since it was high, you could get all the way across the yard and see over the fence opposite the side that Bug had climbed. The area over there was all cemented, with wooden chairs and a table, but nothing was growing in it. What interested Nosey most was a barred window much like their own kitchen window, and she could see someone inside moving pans and dishes around. Nosey felt that she would like to begin attracting attention and getting on good terms with the neighbors.

From that point on the limb she could either go back as she had come or else climb down onto the fence and make her way all around it, looking into her own yard on one side and the three bordering it on the other.

Bug too was venturing further afield now, though she kept a wary lookout for the white cat who had more or less declared himself hostile. Evidently he did not live near, for she saw no more of him for a long time. He proved to come around very seldom, and he never developed into a real enemy. He was only indifferent and unsocial. He only wanted them to keep their distance, and he clearly considered himself in his rights when he walked by. Bug and Nosey soon understood that fences are public property, a kind of freeway along which any cat may pass on his way somewhere else or simply for a stroll if he chooses. Over a period of time they saw that three or four different cats were in the habit of passing by here, some good-tempered and some not. Bug always harbored a feeling of resentment toward the white fellow, since he had given her that first scare.

Now that they had learned to go over the barriers, there was nothing to prevent their pushing on from yard to yard as far as the yards continued. Once outside their own, they were beyond Ann's reach, and she could not hinder them from doing anything. Apparently Ann could not climb the fences. But she could not rescue them either. So they were fairly prudent in their ventures, as most kittens are—although, as they discovered, prudence does not take care of everything. For now a frightful thing happened that made their lives wretched for weeks to follow.

One bright morning in May, just right for sleeping in the sun, they both climbed over into the yard Bug had first visited, and found themselves a sunny spot, for there were no trees there, and they had never seen any people there either. They curled up together in a perfect nook between two wooden boxes of plants, and were deep in a pleasant sun-nap when they were jolted awake by an awful noise. It was like a nightmare. Crouched between them and the side they had climbed over was a large, bushy, dirty gray-and-white-splotched cat with a huge head, fierce, evil-looking eyes, and one ear a chewed, twisted stub. Bug and Nosey could not believe in this creature at first sight, but their instincts were working already, and they were scrambling up and over the other

side as if jerked by strings. There in a strange yard they dived underneath a pile of old boards and tucked themselves back into the smallest possible cranny. Then they heard that fearful noise again, a deep, hoarse yowl, not like any cat noise they had ever imagined. By great luck the hole that they had wedged into was too small for this huge fellow, but they could see his vicious paws and his large, dirty white nose poking in, then an eye glaring through a crack, and there were sounds of scratching and sniffing along with those low, fierce growls. Both their small hearts were pounding hard enough to burst their chests. They did not stir, once they had jammed themselves back as far as they could, and scarcely breathed, but they feared that their beating hearts were making enough noise to be heard. And now began that eternity of waiting for their end—it could have been a half hour or many hours or days. While Bug and Nosey huddled there, they did not know whether night passed over them or how many meals they might be missing. The time in which you wait for your last moment cannot be measured. Days and years mean nothing by comparison. But finally terror, like anything else, becomes a way of life that you get used to. Not that it wanes, but it comes to seem normal.

So Bug and Nosey got used to their terror during the long, long time they sat listening to the scratching over their heads, the soft padding around, and some small pieces of lumber falling off. And now far away, like an echo of their long-ago happy past, they could hear Ann's voice calling and calling, "Kitty, kitty, kitty!" It seemed fantastic that within hearing distance of that past, so innocent and heavenly, they must huddle here awaiting a violent death.

At last they heard no more noises. Their enemy was likely crouched at the end of the lumber pile expecting them to venture out, but they were not to be tricked by that. So their hearts ticked the time away and they waited endlessly—they hardly knew what for, since the less they could hear, the more wary they had to be. And yet, sooner or later, they would have to take the risk.

Ann was sitting in the canvas chair with her papers, worrying about those vagrants who had been missing for two hours—not two days or weeks, though only she had any way of knowing—when she saw two dirty little paws appear at the top of the fence; then a very subdued and shrinking Bug, covered with dust and debris, came creeping over, and, not even stopping for Ann's eager greeting, sneaked into the house and back under the bed. A little while later Nosey came slinking home in the same way, followed Bug back to the farthest corner, and collapsed. There, snuggled close together, they slept in exhaustion.

But that was not the end of their peril. From now on for days they lived a fearful life. All their happy freedom and security had vanished. They saw now that they had never been safe at all. Even in their coziest moments, cuddled by their mother and sucking her milk, their safety was an illusion. All that time the unexplored open space contained big fighter cats with evil eyes and chewed ears who lay in wait to spring upon them. And the inside was really no safer because through the very opening their mother had gone out the fighter cats might invade.

Bug and Nosey did not dare to go outside now, especially at night. They knew the fighter cat was hanging around—sometimes they heard those hoarse, terrifying yowls coming from far or near. The whole neighborhood seemed under siege. Once they saw another cat go slinking by on the fence, and they knew that it too was frightened of the besieger. Ann fixed a sandbox for them in the corner where they had had it when they were tiny, so that they need not go out to the garden. This gave them great relief.

They did not play any more, for they were afraid to be off guard or to make any noise, even in the house. They crept around underneath the couches and were very quiet. At mealtimes they came out, but Nosey did not dare to make her usual noise while their food was being got ready. She barely whispered her meows.

Ann sympathized very much, but the astonishing thing was that she could not really protect them. She could not get rid of the fighter cat. If it came by, she would run out to drive it away, but Bug and Nosey knew quite well that it had not gone far away. It could come back at any time, and the worst of it was that it might come when Ann was not there, for she went out every day to do the many things that must be done by somebody in a household. Sometimes she stayed only long enough to get the groceries, but other times she stayed much longer, and while she was gone, they were terrified. In reality, she left them safe enough. The back door was open, but the iron door outside it was closed, and though Bug and Nosey were still small enough to get through the ironwork of this door or under it, a grown cat was too big. But they did not realize this fact, and if they heard a yowl in the distance, they expected to see the fiend come stalking straight in upon them. So they spent all their time hiding, not making a sound. Ann made a place for them far back in the closet. She put a folded blanket among the shoes and boxes and left the door ajar, and there they usually fell asleep and passed the time when she was away. But they never slept a deep, safe sleep any more. It was always light, jumpy, and full of vague dreams about scrambling up fences just out of reach of some great beast with gigantic teeth and claws.

Now they understood that there must be two ways of life. On the one hand, there is your soft, furry, loving mother who will give her life to defend you. There is your home and somebody like Ann who gets the food ready and keeps everything comfortable. But on the other hand, there must always be some monster who roams the outside world, threatening you and forcing you to be intensely awake and on guard, to keep your wits sharp, to flee or to fight. When you are big enough, you must cope with it. But until then you bide your time and try to evade it.

Days and days passed with nights and nights in between, and they scarcely ventured to poke their noses out the door. They saw other cats go creeping past as if expecting to be attacked. Bug and Nosey took it for granted that the future would always be like this, that they would never be able to run up the trees any more, but would always live in fear, cringing under furniture and whispering their meows.

Still, after a long time all this began to change a little

—they didn't know just how. They didn't hear the terrible yowls for a day or two. One night it rained heavily with flashes of lightning and crashes of thunder. Bug and Nosey slept snug and dry at Ann's feet. The storm was frightening, but a sort of relief from their other fear, for they didn't think that their old tormentor would be out in such weather. In the morning the rain was finished, and bright sunlight shone through the windows. Ann opened the door. The air was clean and sticky and fresh-smelling. The kittens ventured out on the step. They simply couldn't believe that there was anything very bad out there, and they yearned to stretch their muscles, which ached from being cramped so long. Bug had a strong urge to run up a tree, and suddenly she shot like a streak across the wet earth and up a trunk to the first limb. Nosey followed. They both felt liberated. They walked out Nosey's special limb to the fence, and from that point of view they could see Bug's first acquaintance, the unsocial white cat, who seemed almost a friend after what they had been through, sitting on the fence across two yards, washing himself placidly in the sun, seeming quite at ease.

Things had changed. The air seemed cleared of danger. The fighter cat must have left their neighborhood to find himself a new territory.

# Chapter 4

# *A Few Social Contacts*

*N*ow that their besieger was gone, they dared to explore again. They were growing up and their interests were broadening. Nosey was cautiously making a friend.

Early in the morning before Ann woke, Nosey would slip out the window—they were too big now to squeeze through the iron door—and sit on the fence for a few minutes sniffing the new air, which at that time of day always carried a special smell from blowing across water and trees. Then she would stretch, sharpen her claws on one of the pickets, and walk along past three gardens to a place where there was cement and a sort of small stove built of bricks with an iron grill on top. Around this stove there were usually tongs, long forks, bits of charcoal, frying pans, paper plates, chairs, and a pleasant smell of burnt meat. Nosey loved to sniff around here to see if she could find a bite of anything good that might have been dropped the night before. She enjoyed poking into things at this hour before many people were stirring in the houses. Then she would jump up onto a certain window sill where a kitchen window was always open, and inside a man was sitting at a table having breakfast. He was a tall, strong-looking man with a pleasant, cheerful black face, and he always looked pleased to see her. Best of all, he was usually eating sausages. Nosey could smell them from outside, and it was this odor that first tempted her to jump up on the window sill. She was shy the first time, and when he came to the window, she leaped down. But he tossed a bit of sausage out to her, and she found it very tasty. So after a few days, she was glad to take a nibble from his long, black fingers. Still, she wouldn't go inside through the bars, though she was apparently invited.

One morning he was late and leisurely about his breakfast and hadn't started to fry his sausages yet when Nosey arrived. She saw them lying on the table near the window, three nice little ones, and she waited while the man shuffled around his kitchen, yawning and humming a tune along with the tune that came loudly from his radio in the next room. Then he shuffled off to turn the radio down. Now there sat Nosey on the window sill, and there lay three little sausages unguarded a mere jump away. She made a quick leap onto the table, snatched a sausage, and was out again running along the fence, all in an instant. She had only meant to get one, but quite unexpectedly she had three, since they happened to be all strung together in a row, and they bumped along against the pickets as she ran. Safely away, she looked back to see if anything was happening behind her, but nothing was. Perhaps the man didn't know yet, and there was not a thing he could do when he found out. So she jumped in her own window dangling the sausages. Ann was there getting their breakfast ready, and she was shocked to see what Nosey had done. But there was nothing she could do either except to fry the sausages for both Nosey and Bug.

That was the first of Nosey's pilferings, but she decided it would not be the last. Still, she did not go back to that place for a while. Instead, she prowled around to see what other kinds of places there were in the neighborhood, noting the accessibility of windows, but she was prudent and did not approach any of them or try to make any new acquaintances yet.

She and Bug eventually found how far they could go in both directions. For a long time they thought the yards were endless in number, for beyond each one there was still another, a little different and intriguing to investigate. Some were clean and well kept with trees, flowers, shrubs, and ivy, and sometimes people sat there in reclining chairs. Others were abandoned—nothing grew in them, and there were pieces of trash, junk, and rotting lumber lying around. Bug and Nosey liked both kinds. A well-kept yard is pleasant, but they were shy of people. And they did love to poke around in an old trash can to see what they could find. There was never anything that they wanted, but they examined each object as if trying to figure out what it was for.

The kind of yard they were most cautious about was the kind that contained a dog. They had discovered three of these so far, at first terrifying but fascinating. A dog seemed the most awful of creatures, whether it was a huge, shaggy, deep-voiced fellow or a little yapping, senseless puppy. But they soon learned a thing or two about dogs, and saw there was no need to go around trembling over them. In the first place, a dog cannot climb a fence. This is one reason why board fences create such ideal conditions for cats. A fence facilitates everything a cat wishes to do, but it hinders all the activities of dogs. For a cat, a fence is a natural highway to wherever it wants to go. For a dog it is a barrier. Furthermore, you soon see that the dog is not in the yard all the time, and it is such a noisy creature that you can always hear it coming even before a door is opened to let it out. So there is time enough to get away if you have been doing a bit of snooping in the dog's territory. A dog is never subtle, and it does not take you by surprise.

Anyway, for a long time Bug and Nosey thought that the area for their wanderings was limitless, but before the summer was over, they had found both ends of it, or rather they had found the limits beyond which they had no desire to go. This too was a box, a large, irregular box including a certain number of buildings and yards. At one end it all stopped at a stone wall over which some shrubs and trees were growing. They could get on top of the wall easily enough and look down into a shadowy cement area below, with tall buildings rising up beyond. The wall was jagged and steep and seemed to go far down. They felt no urge to try it, although they knew that some cats did climb up and down that wall. The fighter cat must have come that way, and Bug had watched the unsocial white cat do it. He had certain footholds on broken places, which he seemed to know well, and with the help of a ledge or two, he found it a simple matter. When he reached the top and walked past Bug, he paid no attention to her, but she hissed just to remind him of their first encounter.

At the opposite end of the block, everything came to an end at another wall, a cement one, which also dropped into a deep area, and no cat could manage this, for it was too smooth. Beyond, a similar wall rose facing it; they could see people's heads passing along above this and hear an irregular roaring noise. So this was the range they lived within, and it suited them perfectly. It had endless possibilities and variety. All the right furnishings for a cat's life were there. Nosey was more attracted to the social aspects, but Bug preferred solitary adventures.

After a suitable period of time had passed, Nosey thought that she might go back to see how her sausage friend was getting along. She wondered if he still had breakfast at his usual hour, and one morning when the air was especially nice with a kind of crisp touch that made her think she smelled sausages frying, she ambled down that way. She approached quietly, not feeling too secure, and when she jumped up on the window sill, she crouched there a while without calling attention to herself. The man was standing at his stove, and finally he turned and saw her. He grinned.

"Thief!" he flung at her. But he seemed to understand just how a cat would feel when left alone in the presence of three sausages. So he gave her another bite to assure her that they were still on good terms. Then he scratched around her ears, and both were delighted. Nosey saw that she was welcome to come in, and after that, since his window was open most of the time whether he was there or not, she would go in and make herself at home on the couch. She liked the entertainment there. Often in the evening the man's lady friend came in and cooked, and if Nosey was around, she usually got some of whatever there was. Afterwards the two sat on the couch and watched the television. Nosey had no television at home, and she became quite attached to this one. She was fascinated by the little moving figures on the glass rectangle. She sat on the couch beside her hosts and followed those shadowy waverings with wide eyes. Then suddenly she would spring on top of the box, reach her paw down over the glass, and try to capture the elusive shadows. The man and his lady friend laughed more at Nosey than they did at the television without Nosey, and were pleased enough to have her there.

Once every week or so more people came in, and then they cooked on the brick stove outside, and the smell of steaks floated out over all the neighboring yards while the people sang songs and someone plucked a guitar. Nosey and Bug came to look on, for it is exciting to watch a party from a fence. Bug was reserved. She sat delicately and waited to be offered a bite. But Nosey considered herself a guest and did not scruple to solicit all she wanted. She liked knowing people and feeling accepted. It was convenient besides to have a place or two to go for a visit when she was out strolling in case it should happen to rain and she needed a shelter. She began to pay calls here and there to see what other social opportunities there were.

Ann always found her a funny little cat. She thought that if Nosey were a human, she would be the kind who is always going visiting, drinking tea, and telling the neighbors about each other. And then she would come away absent-mindedly forgetting her handbag with her keys and shopping list. Nosey did indeed have a way of looking, as she dawdled along the fence, as if she were going shopping and had forgotten what she needed.

# Chapter 5

# *A* Great Mystery

*A*utumn came, and the cool, windy weather made Nosey and Bug feel lively. The leaves fell, swirling around in the air and making a little trotting noise along the pavement as they ran in flocks. The sky through the bare top branches between the two rows of buildings was bright blue, and there were the cawing calls of birds gathering together.

The two kittens were nearly grown now. They were lovely cats with deep, plushy black fur, clean white breasts and toes, and neat figures. A new and disturbing sensation was beginning to come into Bug's life. At first it made her feel strange and uneasy. Something was burgeoning inside her that felt as if it wanted to burst, and it made her uncomfortable all over. It made her move in an odd way, as if dragging herself, and she uttered some unusual sounds. She needed something, but she didn't know what. She kept being drawn outdoors as if invisible strings pulled on her, but there was nothing special to do out there, and she would come back in. Sometimes the pulling was so strong that she was drawn away from her home, but when she got down nearly to the end of the block, her home would draw her back again. She was restless and bewildered.

Then off in the distance something began to answer her longing. One night she heard a faraway cat yowl, and then another of a different tone. She listened intently. Nobody else noticed, since the sounds were so far off, but then they had nothing to do with Nosey or Ann. Bug knew in her core that two strange male cats at the farthest reaches of the fence were calling to her to leave her home and come away with them. She was frightened. She crept back to the corner under the bed and crouched there, listening. They were still distant, but they would be drawn to the right house, for they sensed that strange, bursting thing in her, and it pulled them too. Now Bug felt a great yearning, but she was afraid.

She stayed quietly back in her corner. The sound stopped for a long while, but she knew the strange cats were still there. Ann went to bed, and Nosey curled up peacefully at her feet as usual. Now it began again much nearer. Nosey awoke with a jerk and listened. It was always disturbing when some new cat came into the vicinity, but now that they were grown, they were no longer so timid. She did not know what these cats were yowling about, but she didn't feel concerned.

Bug knew. Something awesome and wonderful was waiting for her, a great adventure out in the wilds of night, and it was only for her, not for her comrade Nosey. She felt that all the dark outside was humming with vitality especially for her. In all its crevices it knew about her. It knew that her time had come to enter the great mystery of union so that more life could be created to thrive and grow. There was a great tough power out there that would never let life die out, and Bug's time had come to join its big drive.

Now the two male cats were snarling at each other, for each one wanted to be the first to lure the new member into the mystery. And far off a third call could be heard. There would be a great fight, for that was a necessary part of the life drive. Bug shrank with fear, but she knew that she must go out there to meet her callers. Still, she delayed, and the night wore on while the three cats slowly converged. One had a deep bass voice, another a shrill, almost human one. At last Bug knew it was time. No matter how dangerous the night had become, she wanted to go and find out what her part in this drama would be.

She leaped softly up on the kitchen window sill and sat for a while looking out. There was moonlight, and the air was sharp and cold. She could see a grayish spot at the corner of the fence. Now she felt the thrill and the daring. She was ready.

She slipped out between the bars, made a light spring up onto the fence, and moved slowly along it until she knew that a strange cat at the corner could see her. And there she sat for a while doing nothing. From farther down she heard the deep, throaty, yearning call of a still unseen one. They all held their positions for a time, and then the one farther away began to move in. Soon she got a look at him. He was a big black fellow with a white face. The third one with the shrill cry had not yet appeared.

Step by step she became acquainted with her wooers. She felt an intense interest in them and a deep eagerness mingled with joy and terror. She could never have dreamed of having three fierce creatures like these waiting on her, longing for her to come. She was filled with daring, and yet she felt timorous and shy, not knowing what to do. She waited for them to make all the moves, but as the night wound up to its climax, she was drawn most to the big black fellow with the white face, and she knew inside her body that he was the strongest.

Ann and Nosey were both awake, now that the noise was quite near. Ann was anxious about Bug, fearing she might be lured off and not find her way home again. Nosey felt a great curiosity to know what was going on. She slipped off the bed and leaped up to the window, but she could not see much from there. The cold air now had the smell of early morning in it, a time when she often felt restless, and after a while she stole out to see what was doing in this wild and secret dark. She prowled around warily, investigating the adjacent yards until she had pretty well located all the cats. None of them paid the least attention to her. Nosey had never felt herself so overlooked. She could see Bug not far away, sitting by herself in a neat little huddle, from time to time washing one of her paws in a casual manner. Nosey was amazed to see her sister sitting there at this hour trying to pretend that she was quite used to being the center of so

much attention. The black cat with the deep voice was the one nearest her now, and Bug knew it very well, though she didn't throw a glance in that direction. Another was near too, and she knew that also. The third one was still invisible. But things were shaping up.

Meanwhile Ann was lying awake worrying. She dozed off, but later she woke again to hear the strange, wild, high singing of the cats. Their voices rose together, higher and higher in a long, ecstatic wail, and then slowly dropped down to silence. The first dim light of morning made the windows gray. Then there was a little thump on the foot of the bed—it was Nosey, ready to finish her night's sleep. Ann was wondering whether Bug would stray off with all those new companions and be lost and abandoned in some other neighborhood, like her roving little mother, when she felt another soft thump by her feet. There was Bug. Her wild night was over, and she was dead tired. She curled up and fell asleep at once.

Much later in the morning she woke for her breakfast, but after that she slept heavily the whole day. All was quiet outside along the fences. Her friends were evidently resting too in preparation for another moonlit night. Bug forgot about them completely. She only wanted her sleep.

When evening came, she woke and stretched. She felt very well. It was time to eat and take a little fresh air. Dark was already falling, and there was a nipping wind blowing the dry leaves in flurries around the garden, while stars were popping out in the jagged strip of sky above. A big moon, fuller than last night's, was rising over the angle of a roof.

The courting was more exciting this time, and did not take so long getting started, now that they all knew each other. She wasn't afraid, for all the males were in love with her, and when she heard their calls begin at the far end of the block where they climbed the rough stone wall to get into this area, she was waiting. They would be ferocious to each other and fight viciously for the love of their beautiful lady cat, but they would not hurt her. So now it began, and all the potent dark was stretched tight with longing. Again she had her night of intense adventure climaxed by an hour of ecstasy, and when morning came, she slept, peaceful and exhausted, at Ann's feet.

That day while she slept, a gray November mist spread over the sun until the brightness was gone and there was only a fuzz of diffused light. The mist grew as heavy as a gray cloud, and then a dull drizzle set in. When Bug woke, it seemed nearly night already, for everything was a leaden gray outside. Ann was away doing all those things that have to be done, and Nosey was curled up on the couch. Bug stretched herself, sharpened her claws on their scratching board, and jumped to the window sill. Rain was splashing on the concrete outside and thudding onto the dead leaves and sod. The sound of wetness penetrated to her bones. Lights from the many windows around glistened on the wet, bare branches and board fences. Bug hoped that her friends would all stay home. She did not want romance in this weather.

Ann came in with some liver for their dinner, and while she was cutting it up, suddenly Bug cocked an ear very slightly. She heard a far-away yowl. She could tell that it was Gray Boy, for now she knew all their voices.

After dinner she crawled back under the bed. She did not want to go out. But they were coming for her. She heard the high voice of the shy one, and then the deep, mellow call of Big Tuffy, the one who cared most about her. She knew that he was her real lover. He was gentler and calmer than the others, and his yearning voice was so deep that it seemed to come from somewhere far inside him, even farther than his center—from somewhere back beyond, from the great cat spirit that drew all cats together at such times as this as if contracting itself with a great cosmic spasm. He loved her the most, and his love would last longer.

Bug knew she would have to go out in the rain, but she waited. When the others had gone to bed, she sat in the window tasting the raw-edged air and hoping that the drizzle would stop. It never quite stopped, but it hesitated, and she slipped out into a fine, spitting mist. Nosey saw her go, but tonight had no curiosity, snuggling warmly into a hollow place in the blankets. Now Bug felt the excitement rise again. Romance in a cold rain took a special daring. Even the world of sodden earth and dripping shrubs, of wet cement and decaying wood, was vital with this vast urge that surrounded her, of which she was the node. Now she despised the safe coziness inside. Her real life was here in the outer darkness.

In the morning when Ann got up, Bug had not come home yet. The rain had stopped, but the sky, air, ground, and buildings all had a colorless, dirty look. Grit and mud seemed the texture of the day. Nosey had her breakfast alone, while Ann looked anxiously from the window.

After a while a very disreputable Bug came plodding slowly and wearily along the fence. All her beautiful white spots were grimy and muddy, her lovely paws, about which she was always so dainty, were bedraggled. She might have been rolled in a gutter. And she was so tired, so tired of it all. She did not want any breakfast. She did not want to be petted or pitied. She only wanted to crawl back into the closet among the shoes and be left alone to sleep.

Bug's romance was over that day. In the afternoon her three friends came for a farewell visit. No longer fierce to each other, they sat peacefully in a row on the fence and called to her now and then in coaxing, friendly tones. Ann had her first good look at them. Big Tuffy sat nearest, behind him the neat gray one, and lastly, at the corner, was a shy brown and white fellow. Bug was finally aroused, and she cleaned herself up a little, taking her time about it. At last, having regained some of her natural dignity, she strolled out to sit with them. It was pleasant. They were all nice to her and to each other. The sun came out dimly, and they took a walk along the fence, Bug very ladylike though still a bit dirty.

In the evening the three male cats went off, and two of them came no more. But her big black friend, who probably lived a block or two away, did not abandon her. He liked her very much, and seemed to understand that something would come of all this; so every few days he strolled back to see how she was. Bug too probably knew that an important event was to come. But she gave no sign of it for so long that the whole affair seemed forgotten. A month passed, and it was the dead of winter before she began to swell up and get ready for her family.

## Chapter 6

# *The Most Important Business on Earth*

*N*ot that there was much to do by way of getting ready. All she needed was the box in the corner with a blanket in it, and Ann took care of that. In fact, Bug didn't even know what the box was for. She paid no attention, and when Ann put her in it and patted the blanket down, she clearly had no notion what all this was about. Ann thought that she would recognize the purpose of the box later, but Bug never did, even when her time drew near.

One night Ann woke and heard a soft pussyfooting around the floor, accompanied by two or three of the husky, tender sounds that Big Tuffy usually made to Bug. He was in the room. He had never come inside before. Ann listened while he padded around, and then she heard him over in the corner where the box was. She got up and turned on a light. There was the big fellow sitting in the middle of Bug's box, his large head with its startled round eyes and white nose thrust out, while Bug sat perfectly still outside it, watching him. He was certainly trying to tell her that this was the place that had been fixed for her to have their kittens in. But Bug didn't understand.

She was polite to Big Tuffy, but now she liked a certain formality between them. She wanted him to stay at a respectful distance. As for Nosey, the old kittenhood friendship between the sisters was changing, never to be the same again. Bug would not romp with Nosey any more. It made her furious when Nosey came pouncing upon her like a silly kitten, wanting to roll over and over with her as they had always done. Bug would burst into spitting and hissing like a string of firecrackers and strike rapidly with her paw. Every day she grew more touchy until she was having fits of rage against poor, bewildered Nosey, who could not grasp the fact that Bug was grown up now, she was going to be a mother, she had different interests. With no comrade and nothing to do, with the long, dull winter outside and windows closed all around the neighborhood so that she could not easily go visiting, Nosey became bored.

Snow fell in the yard, then melted, then froze. Rain fell and froze and melted. Then nothing except cold days with no sun. Then a little sun. All this went on and on.

Bug felt clumsy now with her swollen middle, and she was careful when she went out for her walks, for often everything was slippery or slushy, and she could not scramble with the same agility as before. The opening in the window had to be made a little wider for her, and she could no longer squeeze through all her favorite holes in fences. But her muscles were strong, and except for the bulge her body was still trim and lithe.

Ann stayed home as much as possible, for Bug wanted her there and would utter anxious little sounds if she saw Ann getting ready to go out. They were waiting for the event, and it came at last one night when snow was falling in little wet wads that stuck on the windowpanes. Bug came in from her late walk, her plushy fur glittering with mist, and was licking herself dry on the couch when there was a spasmodic movement in her distended stomach. She stopped in surprise and then went on with her drying. Another spasm came and then another. They did not hurt her, but they made her uneasy. Bewildered, she went to the kitchen and crept back into a corner under the sink. There on the cold linoleum she prepared to have her kittens. Ann came and stayed beside her, stroking and encouraging her. After a while she brought the box out there and gently coaxed Bug into it just in time for the first kitten's arrival. Bug was surprised to find that the box was just what she needed. A moment later she was too busy to think, and luckily there was no need to think, for all at once she knew everything. All feline knowledge from the beginning of time was in her. The strong, tough spirit of life was in her, hovering over those pitiful things about to be born, and it guided every move she made, filling her with love and power. What a busy mother she was for a while! As each kitten was born, she washed its face rapidly so that it could breathe, then washed it all over until the slime was cleaned away, and finally she chewed the cord in two and freed it to latch itself onto one of her nipples. All this had to be done very fast so that she would be ready for the next. The only sound she made was a little panting when she rested for a few minutes between the arrivals. Meanwhile Ann carried the box back to its proper corner without Bug even noticing the move.

All this time Nosey was filled with curiosity. She did as much sniffing around as she could manage, but Ann kept gently pushing her aside. Nosey had long recognized that Bug was a more advanced cat than she was and that of late Bug was always doing things that she couldn't understand. She did not mind being the lesser cat, since she had few ambitions, but she was left lonely and in the dark about everything. She noticed an odd smell in that corner, and there were some strange tiny cries that sounded like nothing she had ever heard before. All the while Bug seemed to be working so hard that she could not pay the least attention to anything else. Nosey couldn't imagine what she was finding to do back there, but the whole business seemed risky to her.

When it appeared that Bug's family had all arrived and were comfortable, Ann went to bed. In the morning when she came to look at them, Bug was rested and happy. Stretched out and purring, she looked up with a dreamy expression of perfect contentment. The nights of excitement and romance on the fence were forgotten, for now she had the supreme happiness—her three tiny young fastened against her, making little sucking noises as they drew their life from her milk. Their fur was dry and fluffed out. Two were black and white, one marked like its mother and one with a white face like its father.

The third was gray in honor of Gray Boy. Brown Boy was not represented.

Bug got up for breakfast and then went out for a quick stroll. While she was gone, Nosey took the opportunity to have a peep inside that mysterious box. She approached it very cautiously, but one look and sniff were enough. She did not even quite see what was there, but it did not appear worth all the fuss and toil that Bug had been going through. In any case, it was Bug's affair and not hers.

After that she stayed away from the box and tried to amuse herself, since Bug paid no attention to her any more and was always completely occupied back in that corner as though she were running the most important business on earth.

# Chapter 7

# *A Modest Little Affair*

*B*ig Tuffy still came to call sometimes, but Bug did not welcome him now. If she found him on the fence, she snarled and struck at him. She meant him to know that his part in this business was finished, at least until another time, and she would have no unauthorized cats hanging around, no matter who they were. Once she caught the white cat, her old semi-enemy, in the yard, and she lunged at him in such a wild, clawing fury that he scrambled over the fence without even looking back to see what had attacked, and nothing more was seen of him for months. The white cat had not come to Bug's romance. He was indifferent to romance as to most other things.

Big Tuffy was level-headed about Bug's mood. He seemed to understand how it would be with her at this time, and he made no attempt to impose. But now a friendship was developing between him and Nosey. Nosey would go out to meet him, they would touch noses, and ramble off together down to the end of the block, where Big Tuffy showed her how he got into and out of this area by climbing up and down the stone wall. Nosey did not care to try it herself. Her world was big enough, and anyone from the great outside who wanted to see her would have to find his way in.

But she was growing fond of Tuffy. It might even be said that she was acting a little silly over him. Sometimes she would frolic in front of him and then roll on her back and stretch her arms backwards toward him as far as she could reach, and he would look at her kindly, liking all this well enough, but not really overwhelmed by it. He would touch her with his paw and make his deep, loving sounds far back inside himself, letting her be as silly and familiar as she liked, but he retained his dignity, almost a kind of majesty, while sometimes looking toward the windows to see if perhaps Bug was there. When Bug did appear, he kept his distance, knowing she wanted nothing to do with him. Nor was she interested in his and Nosey's carryings-on. They could indulge in whatever nonsense they liked. Her life was focused now on the business of raising a family. She had responsibility.

Nosey was plainly a little in love. The weather was very cold now, but she endured the cold for Tuffy's company. She would sit in the window every morning watching for him, and when he came striding into view, she would scoot through the small opening and go bounding out. It all seemed innocent enough, since Big Tuffy did not lose his head over her. He was an old-timer who had been around and seen a great deal of life, and he knew that this was nothing to get terribly serious about. But it is always nice to have somebody sitting at a window to watch for you and come running out to meet you as soon as you appear. Nosey made him feel welcome. He did not want to romp himself—he was not exactly a young fellow —but it entertained him to see this silly little female romping and showing off around him. It gave him an excuse to come and kept him from feeling discarded.

One night a strong, stinging cold wind came up, and fine snow began to whiz slanting through the air. When they went to bed, the ground was white. Ann woke in the middle of the night and got up to look out. Snow was piled high on the window ledge outside, and the fence pickets were peaked with white caps. The wind made a high singing sound, and the air was so thick with whizzing snow that she could hardly see the buildings opposite. It sifted in around the small curtain that hung over the cats' entrance. She went to peek in Bug's corner, where Bug lay cuddling her three tiny ones, keeping them warm and safe. Then she went back to bed, where Nosey curled snugly at her feet. They all had the cozy feeling that comes in the middle of a blizzard at night when one's bed seems the only warm spot in the world.

In the morning the snow was deep in the yard and was still falling so heavily that nothing could be seen except a void of gray and white with some angular streaks of black. Nosey and Bug made a quick trip out and had a hard time getting halfway across the yard. Their feet sank in without touching ground, and their stomachs dragged. They came back soon, their whiskers and fur full of white fluff. After breakfast Bug went back to her kittens, and Nosey sat in the window to watch. She watched a long time, but Big Tuffy did not come. The journey would be too much for him, for he had to cross streets and climb walls, and on the fences the snow would have to be knocked off step by step. Nosey was not too disappointed, since she had no desire to go out herself. Snow fell most of the day until all the familiar landmarks were buried. When darkness came, early and softly, with white piled against black, and yellow lights from windows throwing streaks across it, the snow was still falling, but lightly now, and sometime during the long night it stopped.

The next day was dazzling. Above the sharp edges of buildings the sky was a wild blue, and the white drifts piled against everything glittered with sunlight between shadows. Bug and Nosey both wanted exercise, so they squeezed out through their opening and dived into the snow. It flew up around them, and they went plunging across it in a flurry of powder, racing up the tree trunks and down into the drifts. It was wonderful sport for a few minutes.

The snow and cold weather lasted a long time, and all that time there was no sign of Big Tuffy. Nosey forgot about him. She was not one to sit and mope over a friend if he did not come. She was finding a new interest these days—Bug's kittens.

The kittens had grown into fluffy round balls and were getting restless. They had begun to venture out of the box through the little door that Ann cut for them, and to

explore that side of the room, at first hugging the walls and furniture. But they always knew where they were, and returned to the box for their naps. They always knew too where their sandbox was, and they went to it with great care, being very neat.

Nosey was fascinated by these creatures now that they were moving around. She did not know what they were, nor quite how they should be treated, and once she was thrown into a fright when they came sneaking up on her and tried to get their dinner from her as she lay dozing in a square of sunlight. But she soon decided that they were playthings to be jumped upon and spun across the room. She hid behind doors to leap out on them, or zoomed down from above. When Bug first caught Nosey at this game, she went into a tantrum. The two had not been friends for a long time, but now to find her darling family, which she had raised so carefully, knocked around like balls of yarn was maddening, and she attacked Nosey in an explosion of claws, teeth, snarls, and hisses. After this she lay around guarding her brood much of the time and fiercely defending them from their bumptious aunt.

Bug played with them herself, but she knew exactly how it should be done. A mother cat should wave her tail gently to give the little ones something to leap upon and capture. She should roll on her back, squeeze them in her arms, and bite their throats softly so that they can learn how to assault their enemies when they grow up. She should lie majestically with her paws stretched out in front like a lioness and let them scramble over her, chew her ears, and hide from each other in her nooks. While they swarmed over her, Bug would snatch every opportunity to lick their faces, and finally when they were tired and hungry, she washed them all over thoroughly and stretched out in the middle of the floor to let them eat until they were drugged with food.

Still, the kittens liked their Aunt Nosey too. She was rough, but she gave them a lot of excitement, and they could scare her in turn by nibbling at her stomach. Nosey couldn't understand the meaning of that gesture.

One day Ann noticed that Nosey was bulging slightly at the sides, and a new realization dawned upon her. Nosey was pregnant! How could that be? They had all forgotten her walks with Big Tuffy, and Ann had never taken that affair seriously. It seemed only a cheerful friendship with some frivolous behavior on Nosey's part but perfect good sense on his. Ann had assumed that he came to see his old love, Bug, and amused himself with Nosey to pass the time. And now without warning here was Nosey bulging faintly at the sides. No yowling on the fence, no other callers to compete with Tuffy, no wild nights in the moonlight—just a quiet, domesticated little affair without noise or fuss. Nosey had no big ambitions or passions. She had no secret glamour that worked in the night to magnetize wooers toward her through the darkness. She was content to have a tame little love with the big fellow who came to see her sister, and he was obliging about it. Why shouldn't he be, after all? Nosey was a nice little cat, not a bit jealous, and she was happy frolicking around him in her silly-girl way. She liked to take things easily and not make a big struggle about them.

As far as Nosey was concerned, the whole thing had been a success, and she was perfectly satisfied.

# Chapter 8
## One Creature's Grief

Bug's family were two months old and eating most of their dinner from a saucer, when one muggy night in March there was a familiar-sounding yowl in the distance. Bug listened, her ears slightly slanted back and the pupils of her eyes large and perfectly round. A feeling was stirring far inside her. That sound came several times, and it reminded her of something important—the time was coming around again. Big Tuffy had not forgotten.

Nothing more happened that night, but before breakfast in the morning an electrifying incident took place. Ann stood on a chair to rummage in the top of the closet, and she brought out a black box with a handle. She set this down and opened it, and when the cats came to investigate, she suddenly scooped Bug inside and closed the lid. Then Bug, scratching frantically, felt herself being carried swiftly away to the end of the universe. Crazy with shock and anxiety, she made a great commotion inside. She felt herself rushing and rushing through space, out beyond the limits of everything knowable, and all around her were the strangest and most terrifying noises. Then suddenly the roaring, rumbling, and screeching stopped, the box was set down and opened. In front of her, surprisingly enough, there was still Ann, and there was a strange man in white clothes. They took her out of the box and put her on a metal table. She felt something puncture her back, and after that she knew nothing for a long time.

Much later she awoke very slowly, feeling unable to move. She could scarcely remember anything, and only wanted to be left in quiet. She seemed to have bands and bandages all around her and to hurt everywhere. By the time she was able to take an interest in her life again, she was used to that place and to the people who fed and took care of her. It was peaceful and pleasant there, and every day she felt a little better.

Bug was away for a week. The kittens were able to manage without her now, but they missed her warm, furry stomach and her caressing tongue. They got their paws sloppy when they drank from a saucer because at first they thought it was necessary to stand with their front feet in the milk—even before Ann set it down they would shake their paws in uncomfortable anticipation. Then they snorted and got their noses and whiskers milky. Afterwards they had to wash themselves, and they always toppled over while trying to do it. They would have been glad to adopt Nosey for a mother, but Nosey, in spite of her bulge, had no concept of maternity yet. She was only a rough-and-tumble companion for them and went tearing around without a trace of decorum.

There was one creature who grieved deeply over Bug's absence. He walked the fence day and night calling mournfully for her. What had become of his beautiful mate? It was time for them to love again. He had felt that powerful magnetism through the darkness and answered it with his heart full of passion. And now she was not here. Where could she be? He still felt the pulling from the place where she had been, but it was not the same. He knew she was not there, and yet he could not believe it. His deep voice was heavy with yearning as he walked by. It had soft, begging notes in it that told all the sorrow of the world for lost love. No bird, no human, could have said it more touchingly.

Nosey still cared for her old friend, and she tried to comfort him, though she knew his sorrow had nothing to do with her. Now that the weather was mild, she would go out to the garden, Big Tuffy would jump down from the fence, and they would lie there on the damp earth a little distance from each other for an hour at a time, he making his soft, tender noises to her as if in appreciation of her kindness, or as if half hoping that she might somehow turn out to be her sister. It soothed him to rest near her in this friendly way. As for Nosey, she was a very modest little cat. She was glad to substitute as best she could for his missing beloved.

Ann too longed to ease his grief. On a warm day she opened a window wide, and he came in and lay on the couch for a long time uttering his dovelike sounds. He knew Bug was not there, but he wanted to be in the place where she had been.

One afternoon Ann came in the front door with the black box, and out of it jumped Bug with a bandage around her middle, tremendously excited at being home again. The first thing she discovered was her kittens, and without an instant's pause she began to wash them as if exactly where she had left off a week earlier. Their reunion was just as exciting to the kittens, and Ann saw at once that she would have to shut them away from their mother, for they wanted to nurse, and she wanted to feed them. Bug's enmity for Nosey too took up where it had left off, and Ann had a difficult time keeping them all in separate places.

Bug stayed indoors for two days with her bandage on, so restless to get out that she tried every possible way to escape. At last Ann cut the bandage off, opened the window, and let her go free to walk the fences again, to visit all her old haunts, and to see her devoted wooer, who came eagerly. But something had broken between them. The magnetism was gone. They touched noses and were friendly to each other. But Bug was clearly indifferent. She did not know how he had yearned and waited. And perhaps he too was disappointed. The great mystery was gone. Perhaps after all she was just a nice little cat like Nosey.

## Chapter 9
# More Domesticity

The little black male who was marked like his mother stayed to live with her and keep her company, since she would never have any more, and his name became Purry. Bug loved him and pampered him for months instead of rejecting him as mother cats must when expecting a new family. She washed him and let him pretend to nurse until he was quite a big fellow and until she had slowly weaned herself from the need to be a mother. The other two went away to different homes after Ann had spent busy days telephoning and talking with all sorts of people who might possibly want kittens. When this business was done, it was time to put the box in the corner again for Nosey.

*"No more kittens after Nosey's,"* Ann said. She tried to remember the days before the first little gray-striped cat came, but they seemed so long ago.

Nosey's middle was bigger now, but not as big as Bug's had been, and with so much going on, Ann couldn't remember when that affair had taken place—she had not paid much attention at the time. But at last she did get around to fixing the box, and the same night Nosey stepped into it and had kittens.

The strangest thing about the birth of Nosey's kittens was Bug's reaction. She was outraged. This Nosey, who never grew up, who treated kittens like rubber balls and was a great nuisance around the house—this Nosey taking on the responsibility of raising a family! There she was back in Bug's corner, in Bug's box, having kittens, an act which Bug had assumed only she herself had a right to commit here. She could smell the odor of birth, which she remembered well. She came close and sniffed. Her fur huffed up, and she growled, trying to warn Nosey not to go on with this business. Then Ann put her with Purry into the kitchen and shut the door, and that seemed to Bug the final offense. She, the matriarch, was pushed away and shut out while that addleheaded Nosey took her place. She was shaken and wounded to her core. She crouched where she could get a peep through the door when it opened, and for hours she sat there with that look of shock and resentment on her face. She wasn't going to take this lightly.

She and Purry were shut in the kitchen all night with a rug to sleep on. Bug's resentment grew and grew. Sometimes she growled quietly to herself. In the morning Nosey had two tiny mouse-sized creatures attached to her, and now it was her turn to be the proudest of mothers. Ann had supposed that more would be born during the night, but Nosey was profoundly content with her pair. After all, for a very small love affair that took place in midwinter, she felt the results were highly satisfactory.

Ann opened the kitchen door, and after a moment Bug came stalking in with a sullen air, her little son behind her. The first thing she did was to march straight over to Nosey's corner, which had so lately been *her* corner, and look disdainfully into what had been *her* box, where now Nosey lay nursing her family. Then she spat violently straight in Nosey's face, and having released her hurt feelings in that one gesture, she turned and marched away across the room and lay down, declining to look in that direction any more. Nosey paid not the slightest heed.

Little Purry had watched this, and now he gathered his courage to go cautiously toward the box. He was convinced that something shocking had happened there, something that threatened the very existence of himself and his mother, or at least their whole way of life. He almost lost his nerve when he came near, but he put his small paws on the rim of the box, bravely pulled himself up, and peeped over. He could see nothing except his Aunt Nosey lying there looking perfectly harmless. He had been great friends with her. But now she had done something that made her their enemy. So he did what he thought was the right thing—he spat in her face, then withdrew hurriedly, ran to his mother, and sat down safely between her paws. Nosey was bored with all this spitting. She had her own concerns and could not be bothered. At last she knew about motherhood and what devotion it required. Let them spit.

Bug never became reconciled to having a successor. Several times every day she walked over to the box where the new family lay snuggled and hissed into it. Nosey chose to ignore this nonsense and was not in the least afraid to go out and leave her kittens unprotected. When she was gone, Bug went to look at them, but she did not touch them. What she wanted in her heart was to be their mother herself, and her hostility was only a cover-up to keep anybody from guessing. Secretly she yearned to step into the box and take over.

As for Purry, he helped his mother to play this game for a day or two, but then he forgot all about it and did not go near the kittens any more until they were big enough to try to come out. When he heard them scratching at the walls of their box, he knew that he would soon have playmates, and he was delighted. Before long he was climbing in with them, not only to play, but also to curl up and have a swig of milk for himself. Oddly enough, Nosey did not seem to mind. She was a most loving mother, but she lacked the strong protective instinct that her sister had. So she let Purry do as he liked. She never attacked and drove away strange cats on the fence as Bug continued to do for a year or so. Bug never gave up her position as senior member of the family, and for a long time she felt it was up to her to protect them all. Nosey knew this quite well, and so she left that part of it to her. She knew that when she went out, Bug would guard her little ones and let nothing happen to them.

# Chapter 10
# *T*he New Generation

*N*osey too went away in the black box for her operation, and during the week she was gone some adjustments were made at home. Bug looked around, felt a little surprised and much relieved at this sudden vacancy, and after two days of no Nosey, decided that she was left the undisputed mistress of the family, the sole possessor of her own and Nosey's kittens. And now they all came to her to be mothered. Her resentment melted away; she took them into her motherly arms, stretched out on the floor, and blissfully let them all attach themselves to her. She had no milk, but they were contented anyway, having eaten their dinner beforehand.

Bug relaxed a little more each day and slowly settled into her comfortable supremacy, feeling that at last things had turned out right. She was tranquil and sweet-tempered, all her mother-tenderness flowered. And then, just when things had arranged themselves to suit her and were running smoothly, Ann came in again with the black box, and out of it popped Nosey, meowing noisily with a look of "Where am I?" on her face. It took her no time at all to find out where she was and begin calling her young ones with loud authority. The two kittens came bounding toward her. Bug stood with her back arched, staring wildly. As far as she was concerned, Nosey had stepped out of the picture and wasn't expected back. Now here she was, a complete intruder, stepping in again without a qualm.

It took days for things to settle down once more. All that Bug had taken for herself during that quiet week was contended over and compromised. But at last, with poor grace, she relented and grew indifferent. And now that summer was coming on once more, she began to find other interests for herself. She was tired of indoor life and family matters. She wanted to be out in the open.

They were all glad to have summer, to have the windows and door open and green things growing outside. It had been a busy winter and spring, what with all the love affairs, kittens, operations, and home-finding—for now one of Nosey's also went somewhere else to live. The little all-black female stayed to be a joy and comfort to her fond mother and a playmate for Purry. She was soon named Bitsy, for nothing else seemed to fit her when she was cupped in Ann's hands with all four little black feet up, bright black eyes taking in everything, and the fur on her stomach very fluffy. Bitsy had managed somehow to be almost a long-haired cat.

Purry doted on his little cousin. He would go into

ecstasy over her when they played, but because he found
her so exciting and he tried so hard to show off in front of
her, he usually lost control and grew too rough. He
would start very gently, determined not to scare her, but
soon he was zooming the length of the two rooms and
garden, up and over all obstacles, and if tiny Bitsy did
not take refuge under something, she would be knocked
over and spun headlong. Or he would begin by sweetly
licking her face and then grow too ardent, so that soon
there was scratching and biting and a screech from Bitsy
as she scrambled for cover. Then Purry was pitifully
sorry and would try to lick her face again. Often he was
like a mother to her, cuddling and washing her lovingly,
and they would go to sleep together. He adored his Bitsy,
and though their friendship went through various phases
as they grew older, it never came to an end. They always
loved each other.

They had a joyous life together. When Bitsy grew a
little bigger, they scrambled up and down the tree
trunks, raced around the house and garden, pulled down
everything they could get their paws on and knocked it
around. Purry was eager to show Bitsy the world. He
wanted her to climb the fence and explore the neighborhood with him, but she was still too timid. So he poked
around until he found a weak place at the base of the
fence, and with his strong little paws he dug a hole for
her to go underneath. Bitsy found the hole inviting, and
soon she was familiar with the yard next door where the
ivy beds were. Nobody seemed to object to the hole, so
Bug and Nosey enlarged it, and it became their main
passageway.

Bug was becoming a huntress. She wanted her son to learn to hunt, and so she would go out and bring some little thing back to him. Not that there was much to bring. Often it was just a big, hard-shelled cockroach that she found under some boards, or a mere pigeon feather, which she brought simply as a token of an occupation that he must learn. She loved to go out in the dark early hours of morning and come leaping back over the fence with a special call that meant she had something in her mouth. Purry recognized that call as if he had known it in some primitive pre-existence, and, though sound asleep at the time, he would tumble off his cushion and go tearing outside to his mother, clambering through the ironwork of the outside door. He was very glad to eat the cockroach with much growling or to paw at the feather and carry it around as proudly as if he himself had plucked it from its owner. He liked best to parade back and forth before little Bitsy, who would be sitting at the corner of the house watching, for she too came at the call to see what Purry's mother had brought. She was very impressed when Purry strutted like a big cat in a dangerous world, showing off his fierceness.

Sometimes Bitsy's mother brought her something too, but it usually turned out to be a little sausage, for Nosey preferred daytime hunting at the window of her sausage friend. This kind seemed more profitable. But Bitsy growled and was just as proud, since, for all she knew, sausages had to be chased down and captured just like cockroaches.

Once in a while Big Tuffy came ambling along the fence to have a look at his families and see how they were. Bug and Nosey both treated him well and did not mind if he jumped down and touched noses with the young ones. They were all on good terms and quite peaceable together. But in truth Tuffy was a little bored with the domestic side of it, which really had nothing to do with him. And now that Bug no longer excited him in the old way, his visits became fewer. No doubt he was roaming elsewhere to see if there existed for him in the world another creature like his Bug of the old days.

By the time Purry was four months old, he was having many adventures, for he had great curiosity and plenty of nerve. His one terrible experience came much later when he was grown, and it was so terrible that it nearly cured him of his desire to try things. But while he was still a kitten, he was eager to find out anything he could about this interesting creation that he had been ejected into. The most memorable of his minor scrapes was the time that he got locked into somebody else's house for a whole day and evening without food.

This mishap was due to an early-morning rain. Purry was already out inspecting the neighborhood to see what was doing, and when the rain came with a crash of thunder, he made a streak for the nearest doorway. He found himself under a table in a strange kitchen, and there was a pair of strange plump feet in high-heeled shoes stomping around him. Then suddenly the door was pulled shut, the high-heeled shoes withdrew, he heard another door slam, and then all was quiet. He was caught alone in this place, and he had had no breakfast.

That day Bitsy did a lot of sleeping, having no play-mate. Between naps she looked around for Purry and made plaintive little sounds. Bug too called for her son, hunting in closets and under couches. As for Ann, she put on her raincoat, went out the front door, and walked several times around the block looking into all the little spaces that are to be found in front of houses, around steps, and through iron gratings and gates. She did not think that Purry could have got out into the street, but there was nothing she could do except to look for him there. The long day passed, and when evening came and slowly went by, she decided sorrowfully that he must have met with some accident.

Purry was a hungry little cat, for he had no dinner either. All day he had cautiously investigated the place, especially the windows, but there was no way out, and he thought he would be left here to die. Dark fell and no one came. From time to time he crawled back underneath a sofa and slept a while, dreaming of his home and the food they would be eating there.

It seemed the middle of the night when he was awakened by a noise. Someone was fumbling at the door trying to open it. He heard bumps and mutterings and a key wiggling in a lock. Finally the door burst open and someone half fell into the room. Purry shrank to the wall and dared not move for a few minutes. But more than anything else, he wanted to be found before he starved, so he uttered a few distressed meows. After a sudden stillness, he heard grunts and pantings; someone was getting up from the floor with difficulty. He saw the same two plump legs and high heels he had seen that morning, but they swayed unsteadily. Then a pair of knees met the floor with a thump, and an amazed round red face came

into view upside down. This unusual creature began to
call, "Kitty, kitty!" but she could not see him, so Purry
meowed again. She reached an arm underneath the sofa
and flourished it vaguely, but Purry had emerged and
was under a chair. This oddly unstable person moved
around the room in search of him, but whether crawling
or standing, she had great difficulty. Purry ran from
under one thing to hide under another. It was easy
enough to keep out of her reach, but how was he going to
get himself rescued? She seemed quite heavy, for there
was a great thud every time she went down, and he was
afraid of getting a paw pinched under one of her sharp
heels when she stood up. Finally, still calling to him, she
got to her kitchen, opened the refrigerator, and began to
take out all sorts of things, which she set one by one around
on the floor. Purry approached eagerly and stretched his
neck to see what there was. The first item he recognized
was some tuna fish in a bowl. It turned out to be mixed
with celery and other things he would have preferred to
do without, but he began to gobble it anyway. Then
there were some slices of salami and some hamburger,
not his favorite dishes, but very welcome now. He
snatched about while trying to keep out of the woman's
grasp, since she kept reaching out to pet him, but she was
so top-heavy that she kept falling forwards and knocking
over a jar of pickles or a paper carton of milk. Purry
lapped up some milk from what was spilled. When he
had crammed as much food as he could into himself, he
ran to the door he had come in that morning and
meowed urgently. Plainly her only wish was to oblige
him. She staggered to the door and worked hard to get

the latch undone. While she worked, Purry tried to hurry her by meowing, and she began to meow too in a last attempt to establish some kind of contact with him. Suddenly she fell asleep on the floor. In desperation Purry began to walk around on her, scratching, until she revived and worked at the door again.

Ann was sitting at home with her books under the lamp, thinking that she would never see Purry again, when a little cat face was thrust timidly up over the chair. There was Purry looking bewildered and unsure of himself, not quite knowing whether anyone would remember him. He thought he had been away for a long time, and everything looked unfamiliar. But what a happy homecoming it was!

After that he sometimes went back to see the lady of the high heels, though he would never go inside her house again. He sat near the door and gladly accepted any tidbits she brought out to him. But he declined to be petted, for he was wary of her clacking heels and of the possibility that she might topple over on him, though he was glad to observe that most of the time she was fairly steady on her feet.

## Chapter *11*

# *Hunters, Fierce and Gentle*

Purry's next big exploit was the catching of the mouse. This was a real turning point for him. He was nearly six months old by that time, and afterwards he considered himself grown up. He had never seen a mouse before. His mother, although a huntress, had never caught one, for this was, after all, a fairly proper neighborhood, not the sort where mice are expected to turn up—and yet somehow a family of mice did turn up there. So either the neighborhood was not so proper or else the mice had got there by mistake. The young must have grown up in a safe place underneath some boards in someone's yard, and now they were looking for better quarters. They wanted to be house mice rather than yard mice. And of all the houses in that particular block, they misguidedly chose the one where four cats lived. One managed to work its way under a loose brick at a corner and a bit of

loose plaster, and suddenly one night Purry made a startling leap from the desk by the window and came up
with a squeaking mouse in his teeth. Those squeaks were
its last, for when Ann came in from the kitchen, it was
dead. Purry dropped it and stood there over it as if he
thought himself some huge, fierce beast of the wilds. All
the others came running to see what he had, but none of
them dared get very close. Even his mother kept back,
for he had suddenly emerged from the playful, soft,
babyish creature he had been up till now. All his angles
had turned crisp and proud so that he looked big and
dangerous.

Purry had a wild time with his dead mouse for more
than an hour. He tossed it in the air and caught it. He
strutted through the house and around the yard with it.
He paraded the fences, glaring fiercely to right and left,
hoping that all his acquaintances would come to behold.
In every movement he was daring the world to challenge
him. He wanted to fight over his prey. But no other cats
came, and as for Bug, Nosey, and Bitsy, they followed
him cautiously at a safe distance or crouched around in
corners watching, but they did not challenge him. Finally, after displaying his kill all up and down their
known territory, he came home, followed by the family,
and dropped it on the kitchen floor. There he lay like a
lion with the mouse between his paws, gazing around at
his three admirers, who sat under the tables and chairs
eyeing him. Ann came to join the audience, to Purry's
satisfaction, because he wanted them all to see that now
he had finished growing into his role as the only male in
this establishment. He wished one of them would show

an inclination to try to take his mouse from him, but nobody made any such move. Then he picked it up and marched back and forth in front of Bitsy. He wanted above all to impress her. She sat quietly with her neat little paws folded inward and looked at him with modesty and femininity, dropping her head to one side. Purry was much pleased. But at last there was nothing more to do with his mouse except to eat it, and he did so in front of them until the last morsel, tail and all, was gone. He had never enjoyed any food so much. That finished, he quieted down to his normal mood, washed himself thoroughly, and fell asleep.

He was a big boy from then on. Not that being a big boy kept him from still trying to nurse his mother once in a while. But she was getting a little sick of that now, though all these months she had encouraged him to play the baby because she wanted so much to play the mother.

That was not the end of the mouse story. Still another mouse from the same family found its way into the yard that it should have most avoided. One day Ann was cleaning house and shaking rugs out the window when she heard a piercing little squeak coming from outside. She saw Bug sitting by the fence staring intently at something on the ground. The squeak sounded again, high and agonized. It seemed to come from exactly where Bug was sitting. Ann dropped her rug and ran out to see what could be making such a strange noise, and for the first instant she simply did not believe what she saw. Bug was sitting up on her haunches staring as if she could not believe it either. Before her, with its back to the fence, sat a little mouse, also on his haunches, its

paws held up in front of it like a begging dog's, and its bright little eyes full of agonized beseeching. Then it raised its eyes to Ann, not fearfully, but begging for help. No mouse ever implored mercy so eloquently. Its eyes took in its whole situation: to the cat it was pleading, "Spare my life!" and to the human it was praying, "Save me from the cat!" The three of them, human, cat, and mouse, remained caught in their poses staring at each other for some moments. None of them knew what to do. Bug did not want the mouse. Sometimes her cat instincts were not very strong. Or perhaps she had something above cat instincts. She wanted to allow the mouse to go free, but could think of no way to let it know. As for Ann, her good sense told her: mice should be caught by cats. But at that moment nature seemed suspended, waiting for something else to step in. Finally Ann stooped and drew Bug back from the fence, and the mouse with a little flurry squeezed underneath it and was gone.

Afterwards Bug was haunted for days by the memory of that mouse. She pawed around the spot where it had disappeared. She went over the fence and dug on the other side. She sniffed and pawed along the base of all the fences in the neighborhood and around all the flower boxes and pots. Sometimes she was so occupied with this curious search that she did not come home at meal hours, and when Ann went out to call, her head would come popping up, very alert, and with large, luminous eyes, from behind a fence, where she had been crouched waiting and listening with all her earnestness for that mouse to come back. It would be difficult to say what she wanted with it. But she could not get it out of her mind for a long time.

# Chapter *12*

# *An Invasion from Above*

The squirrels came that year too, but they were not to be daunted by the cats. Far from it, they ignored the cats half the time and made sport of them the rest, for they had all the advantages.

The mother squirrel came first during the summer, making a careful survey of the area to decide whether she could winter there or not. She evidently had her nest and young in a tall tree somewhere between the buildings near the end of this block, having moved up from the park much earlier. What she wanted to find out now was whether there was some dependable place hereabouts for a squirrel to get a fairly regular supply of peanuts. Of course plenty of people will put out a peanut now and then. Some people will even dump a whole bag of peanuts on a window sill at once, and keep a squirrel busy for an entire day carrying them off and packing them into its various hiding places. But then what? These same people may afterwards forget or disappear and never put out another peanut in their lives. The best type is some steady person who is at home a great deal and who lives within easy access of the squirrel.

So this one came along leaping from tree to tree, and she saw down below in one of the gardens a blue canvas chair with somebody sitting in it. There were several cats lying close around in shady spots among green plants, all sleeping lazily. It was easy to see that these cats didn't have to earn their own living. Cats are not much from a squirrel's point of view, but as for people, they can usually produce something that a squirrel can eat, so she began to circle around downwards from the fine, high branches to the sturdy lower limbs. Squirrels can do most things better than cats, but there is one thing they cannot do at all—they cannot move stealthily or noiselessly. So all the way down the tree this one transmitted from her body to the branches a great deal of jerking, twitching, and whisking, and meanwhile all the eyes below were fixed upon her in astonishment. Ann was astonished because she had never expected visits from squirrels here where walls were so close on all sides, and the cats were astonished because they had never dreamed of a creature that might be half bird coming frisking down through a tree like that, swishing a banner of a tail as if to notify the lowly inhabitants of its arrival from space. They were thrown into a spasm of excitement, as much terror as curiosity. They scrambled to all sides—the two smaller ones vanished into the house, and the others crouched to defend themselves against some kind of assault. But the squirrel, having arrived at the lowest limb, suddenly drew herself up, sat back, crossed her paws on her chest, and was absolutely stationary. Purry and Bitsy came creeping to the doorway for another look. While the cats were all trying to adjust themselves, Ann went in and hunted in her cupboard for some suitable refreshment for her new species of caller. She had no peanuts, but fortunately there were some watermelon seeds, and she scattered these at the base of the tree. Then with four cats and one human sitting around to watch, the squirrel moved spasmodically down the tree and sat at its base long enough to crack open and eat two watermelon seeds. The cats looked as if they were witnessing the supernatural, each one crouched on the edge of readiness to attack. But none moved until the squirrel turned with a jerk and leaped back up the trunk. Then Bug, wound up to the breaking point with suppressed excitement, shot after it as if her spring had snapped, and reached the third limb almost instantly. But by then the squirrel was high in the tree making a great racket and commotion among the branches, and a moment later she sailed across to the next and on to the next in joyous contempt for those earth-bound creatures. Then all four cats lost their heads and began to race around. They tore up and down the nearby tree trunks squirrel-hunting until they forgot what they were doing and were merely chasing each other.

The squirrel came back the next day, throwing them into a spasm again. They watched for her every day after that as if they were scanning the sky for an invasion, but they were already getting used to her and accepting her as a part of the known universe. Her visit gave zest to a drowsy afternoon, an event to look forward to and prepare for. She excited them to fits, for they knew of no other creature who could arrive with such flair and who flaunted itself so brazenly. Ann had laid in a supply of peanuts, and every day the squirrel came down the tree trunks and helped herself in cool style, also taking a long drink from a dish of water, though each time she was surrounded by cats who seemed about to close in on her. After eating two or three peanuts, she carried off the rest one at a time and tucked them away somewhere nearby, and as she grew still bolder, she would dig little holes there in the garden and bury them, coming back later to carry them off, and often having to hunt, since she couldn't remember where she had put each one. She made free with the garden, while her every move was watched intensely by four cats. But they had great respect for her. She had sharp teeth and claws and could move with an abrupt speed that always startled them. If they tried to outwit her by maneuvering between her and the trees, she simply sprang up over their heads high onto a trunk. Before long it was understood on both sides that neither really menaced the other. Squirrels and cats have nothing to fight about, since luckily neither cares for the other's food or type of housing. The cats did not begrudge her the peanuts, and they enjoyed watching her eat them—she was so noisy and so intent about it.

But just as they were getting used to her and accepting her in the daily routine, she astonished them out of their minds by bringing along two young ones. These were nearly full grown, and, compared to their mother, who

was shaggy and worn from a busy season, they were plump, glossy, and new-looking. They were at first too shy to come close, but, like kittens who dote on each other, they played, quarreled, frolicked gleefully, and were inseparable. They spiraled around the tree trunks, swung over and under the limbs like acrobats, leap-frogged one over the other's back, and plunged into each other's arms.

The cats lost their heads again. Three squirrels, all in rapid motion, gave the impression that the trees were swarming with them. Until now, it had seemed that only one of the species existed, and anybody can adjust to a species with only one member. But a whole flock of these things frisking over your head would seem to indicate that they, like cats, probably came in at the beginning and were well established. In time it all turned out to be fun, especially for Purry and Bitsy; though two young squirrels and two young cats may not quite come to like each other, they can have a very good time together, and before long all were on playful, teasing terms. When brisk fall weather came with snapping winds and whirling leaves, they were all tight with energy and chasing each other everywhere—but they were most careful never to catch one another.

By now the young ones were tame and took peanuts from Ann's hand as fast as they could get them. When the weather grew colder, she put the peanuts with the water dish on the kitchen window ledge, always leaving a few at night because they liked to come early in the morning, and this remained their regular feeding station. The mother at least had come to stay—it was just the place she had been looking for. This Ann seemed to be all right, since she never failed to put the peanuts out, sometimes with bits of coconuts or seeds. And even if she should forget, the squirrel could rap on a window to remind her. Later on, she came often to the window where she could see Ann sitting at a writing table—not because the peanuts had been forgotten, but because the squirrel felt that the ration might be increased. She tried invading the kitchen to find out where the peanuts were kept—it would save trouble to get at the source. But once when she was pushing under the curtain of the cats' entrance, she came nose to nose with Purry on his way out, and both felt offended. So she gave it up, seeing that awkward situations could develop.

Bug grew attached to the squirrels. She seemed to want to understand them and their way of life. Sometimes she sat quite still on the window ledge, and the mother squirrel came whisking close to her, sitting up as if she expected Bug to give her a peanut. More than once they almost touched noses. With cats Bug was often impatient, perhaps because she could see through them, but she found other creatures interesting.

Winter came. The squirrels loved snow, and on a bright morning after a snowfall they were at their liveliest, trailing in a file up one limb and back another while sprays of glittering fluff showered sparkling around them, and sometimes a pair of gorgeous bluejays hopped on the branches near. But in the middle of winter the two young ones felt a need to gain experience and see the rest of the world. So together they found their way out of the block and down into the park, where no doubt their lives broadened quickly. Their mother had already seen the world. She knew about it and understood that she had a good thing here. So she stayed on and came every day to Ann's window. In the spring she missed coming one day. Ann found the peanuts still there and wondered what had happened to her. But the next morning she appeared early, and she had brought with her a new mate.

## Chapter 13
# Three Are Left

But before that winter and spring came, all sorts of unfortunate things began to happen. Most of them turned out well in the end, and so we may simply call them adventures or experiences. But in Nosey's case, there is nothing to call it except her complete disappearance, and nobody in Ann's house ever found out what had become of her. Of course anything *might* happen to a funny little cat who goes visiting all up and down the block nosing into anything that is available.

Ann always wondered how she got away with so much. Her most shocking theft was a huge sausage tied together at the ends into a ring, which she dragged in and bumped around the floor in the middle of the night. Ann was jolted awake and could not imagine what strange flopping beast had got into her house. She sprang up and turned on the light to behold Nosey with a sausage nearly as big as herself. This was the climax of Nosey's lawless escapades. Since Ann never knew who the sausage friend was or where he lived, there was nothing she could do to make reparation for those burglaries. It was most embarrassing. But the sausage was a nice one, so she coaxed Nosey with a bite of fish to let go of her booty, and then put it into the refrigerator. She fed it to all the cats a little at a time, and it lasted for some days. Nosey would never, she thought, be received at her sausage place again.

But that friendship was evidently a firm one, for Nosey soon presented herself there, was welcomed, and even admired by this man, who respected a good technique when he saw one. He figured that he had been outwitted if Nosey got away with his breakfast or dinner. If you make friends with a bandit, you must be on your guard and not turn your back when your goods are left unprotected. So these two got along and grew to be on affectionate terms. Nosey could come in and lie around as long as she liked, watch the television, and wait in case there should be a little snack of something nice for her. She was always glad when the lady friend came, for the cooking was better then, and she got more attention. Sometimes when the two of them were in the kitchen eating their dinner, and Nosey had had a few bites of fish or steak, she retired to the living room, seated herself in readiness on the couch, and meowed to have the television turned on. The man thought that it ought not to be turned on just for her, but his good-natured, dusky-skinned lady felt that a guest should be entertained, and she would go to oblige.

Once Nosey went to visit her friend when he was getting dressed for what must have been a special date, for he had all his drawers open and was taking out piles of things in an effort to match up shirt, tie, and socks. Nosey loved this state of affairs. There was nothing she enjoyed more than rummaging in drawers to see what they contained. She helped herself to a pair of brown socks that were neatly rolled up in a ball and began to bat it around the floor. Her friend picked it up and threw it to her several times, and suddenly Nosey snatched it and leaped out the window onto the fence just as though she had stolen a piece of fried chicken. The man stared after her as she made off down the fence with his socks. A moment later she popped in the window at home and dropped her prize in front of Ann, who was more astonished than ever at Nosey's strange offerings. The next day Nosey went back to her friend unabashed, nibbled cheese blintzes and pawed at the dresser drawers to suggest that they be opened again.

Now the time has come to end the story of Nosey, though there is nothing to tell except that one morning she was not there, and they never saw her again. Ann hunted and inquired for many days, and long afterwards, on different occasions, she ran across two other black cats in the neighborhood with crooked white spots on the right sides of their noses; but when, after some trouble, she managed to get a close look at each of them, she saw that neither of the crooked white spots was the same as Nosey's. She never had any clue as to what had become of her lost cat. Anything *could* happen to a creature who took so many liberties. Perhaps—and this was what Ann always hoped—the sausage friend had moved away and taken Nosey along with him. He might have decided that she herself must compensate for all her thefts. Or perhaps he was just fond of her.

Nosey was much missed at home. A silly little cat, like a silly little person, is sometimes missed more, at least for a while, than a deep and serious one would be. Bitsy missed being mothered, though she was nearly grown by now. Purry's relationship with his Aunt Nosey had always been a jolly one, and lately she had even had a crush on him. Bug alone was indifferent. Bug had never had much regard for her flighty sister after they grew up, and they had simply ignored each other for a long time. But Ann felt that her family was never quite complete again, and for weeks and months she hoped and half expected to see Nosey come strolling along the fence looking addled and forgetful, as if she had been to tea at a neighbor's and mislaid her handbag somewhere.

## Chapter *14*

# *A Terrible Experience*

*It* was an unlucky autumn. Purry's disappearance followed not long after Nosey's. But Purry came back home ten days later, and so we can report his adventures. Those ten terrible days were more like ten years for Purry, but they were useful, for during that time he learned all he ever wanted to know about the world.

The whole affair began with some workmen pounding on a house four doors away. Purry knew this yard well, and it was one of his favorite places, since it was full of cans and old pieces of junk which were interesting to poke around. So he was disturbed by the hammering that was going on there, for fear it might threaten his prowling projects. It continued day after day, and he went back often to see how matters stood. Bug and Bitsy went too, but they were not so curious about such things as Purry was. One day he found all the back part of the house torn open. Doors and windows were gone; he could look right through the long interior and see light at the other end. This view frightened him. It gave him clear proof that there was space out there on the other side of the buildings. It was like the glimpse he could catch through the hallway at home with a door at the end that sometimes stood open. He always wanted to go out there, but he was never given a chance. Here he could see a big splotch of daylight streaming through a far end, and there was nothing to hinder him if he wanted to go through the building and see what was beyond it. The workmen were pounding as before. But Purry knew by now that they went away in the late afternoon, and after that the place was deserted all night. He tucked the whole thing back in his mind and went home.

That evening at dusk after his dinner with Bug and Bitsy, he wandered up that way and sat on the fence for a while behind the open building. It was vacant. Not a soul was around, and all noises were distant ones. There was nothing at all to prevent a cat from walking into that building and having a look around. He jumped down and moved sneakily, his bones seeming to slide along under his skin, and he paused to sniff everything, even before he got to the building. Now he found himself inside, padding over a pile of rubble—bits of plaster, cement, and brick—and then he was slinking along some boards that made a sort of pathway toward the light at the far end. The place was vast and resounding. When a bit of brick clinked under his paw, the noise echoed. There were no walls or partitions. The place was empty except for rubble, boards, and pipes, which he had to maneuver

around. At last he neared the dusky light. It came from
an open doorway, which he passed through very cautiously. All was quiet. He crept up three cement steps
and found himself in the open. Then he slithered along
beside an iron balustrade for a few steps. After all, he
could always go back—there was nothing to hinder him
—but having got this far, he might as well see once and
for all what there was on this outer side of his world from
which he had been kept. The space around him was bigger than any he had ever seen. He had not dreamed there
was so much room anywhere. Perhaps this was just the
roominess that cats need to conduct their affairs in when
they are grown up.

Suddenly there was a startling noise of people laugh-
ing and talking, and a lot of feet clattered down the steps
of a building just behind him. He leaped forward and was
scrambling as fast as he could down into a dark area
when a door slammed down there, and he bolted up
again. Then a frightful thing happened. A huge black
bulk swept by not more than a few feet from him, making a hideous roaring noise. Purry fled for his life, tearing
in any direction, out of his mind with fright, but before
he could find any kind of refuge along a solid brick wall
another gigantic thing lunged past and then another. The
noise itself was enough to crush him, and he assumed
that his end had come. The next instant he would be
ground underneath one of those roaring things. Leaping
and plunging, he seized the first shelter that offered and
found himself in a long, tight cranny between two walls.
He settled to perfect stillness, but his heart was pounding
so loudly that he was afraid it could be heard every-

where. For a long time he huddled there not making the slightest motion. Every moment or two he heard that roaring noise, and between roars there were many loud footsteps and voices. His heart kept on pounding. Oh, to be back in his own safe yard! Now he saw that this was no realm for cats, and he would never try it again. He would wait here in this cranny until night had fallen and the roaring had stopped, and then pick his way home.

The deep night fell, but the roaring did not stop. It came again and again at uneven intervals, and now there were glaring lights that moved with each roar, seeming to search him out as they moved over him. Other noises had increased too. Swarms of people seemed to be passing by.

Purry crouched there for hours. He did not fall asleep, but he grew numb with stillness, terror, and cold. Still, his hope held out. Sometime the awful uproar would have to stop. All things are bound to quiet down in the dead of night.

The hours passed, dragging heavily. Night can be unbelievably long when you are hiding in a cold place. At last he fell into a stupor, and when he awoke, he could not remember why he had no warm blanket under him. Why was he stiff and cold against a stone wall? Then his awful predicament came back to him. Now it was the dead of night. The noise had quieted down. At least he did not hear those overwhelming roars. He stirred stiffly and came creeping out of his cranny. Hugging the wall, he stole along for a little distance. But now the difficult thing was to judge how far he had come. In his fright he had bolted so fast that he might have covered a lot of

ground. But he wasn't sure which way he had bolted. He wasn't sure which direction he should take.

He crept along, nosing into all the dark little areas where there were steps down to closed iron gates and doors, with spaces for flower tubs, paved with cement or bricks, and openings underneath the front steps. In one of those sunken areas he hoped to find the open door to the big empty building he had come through. He kept going down the two or three steps into those sunken entrances, but everything was closed. He tried the other direction. Meanwhile, every now and then the terrific roar came again, a huge thing bearing down on him with glaring lights, throwing him into a spasm of fright, and each time he hid in the nearest crevice, his heart pounding as before. But it seemed that if you stayed close to the buildings, those things did not crush you.

Purry wandered and hunted all night long, following every hopeful hint. At last the gray daylight began to come. All was sunk in deep quiet. The early-morning cold and a numb weariness saturated him. He was lost. He crawled through a hole in a piece of broken wire grating and found himself against a very dirty closed cellar window. In this tight little nook he curled up and went to sleep. When he woke, sunlight poured aganst the dust-clogged grating, warming his hide-out, and all the mad noises had come back. He decided to stay where he was as long as he could bear it. There was no breakfast for him anywhere. He was a homeless cat.

He huddled in his cramped hiding place most of the day. In the evening he knew that he must try to get something to eat. But the loud clatter of footsteps never ceased, and he dared not expose himself to all those busy people. Still, you might as well die of anything else as of starvation. So he seized a fairly quiet moment to come crawling out and make a quick dash to the next nearest shelter, a low place back under some steps among garbage cans. From here he made another quick dash up onto the sidewalk, and down into another under-the-stairs entrance way, and from here to another. He soon saw that this was getting him nowhere. There was no dinner to be had by scrambling from one hole to another. Meanwhile the rush and roar of great black monsters in the street went on, but now he was getting used to that. At least they were not after him. They might be after each other. If he stayed out of their way, perhaps they would not notice him. As for the people passing by, they did not seem to be after him either, and he began to see that he must make someone aware of him if he was to get anything to eat. But he hadn't the courage to walk right out among all those feet and wheels.

Dark came again. He felt a little safer in the dark. Again he hid in a lower entrance and heard people going up and down the steps over his head. He took a peep and saw that many of them carried brown paper bags in their arms, the same kind of bags that Ann always brought home full of things to be put in pans and cooked, and smelled so good and were so delicious to eat. He thought he could sniff some of those good smells now. If only some window would open and somebody would set a dish of something warm and tasty on a window sill. But nothing like that happened. He was finding out how few people paid any attention to cats. If you know one person who does, it is best to stick to that person. And to think, he had wanted to learn what it was like out here in the world. To think how it must be at home now with everybody eating dinner! This was a very low moment for him. He felt weak and spiritless. He could have died of homesickness.

That night too was an eternity. In those blank, dead hours of early morning, when darkness and silence were deepest, he came out of his latest hiding place, determined that this was the time to save his life if he was going to save it. He could not live in holes without food.

He stole along the sidewalk, bolder now. There were no footsteps to be heard, and so he crept for some distance with a different style of movement. He refused now to be so terrified. He moved stealthily and warily, but with a certain daring, for now he was a hungry animal that wished to survive. Soon he came to a corner where there was a much wider space and a strong, cold wind was blowing. In front of him two roaring monsters rushed by and then two more. But he would not be daunted. He turned the corner and slunk close to a low iron fence along a wall. Between the fence and the wall were bare bushes swished by the wind, and he slipped into these and made his way. He came to another corner and turned. Here the wind was cut off, there were doorways again, and the monsters, instead of whooshing by, were parked quietly between the sidewalk and the space where they liked to race along. He was learning the habits of these things now, and found them harmless when they were still.

Suddenly there emerged from under one of them a thin dirty gray cat. It crossed the walk in front of Purry—he could see it plainly in the street light. He stopped short, his back drawing up, and watched it. It picked its way up some steps to a front door, where it nosed around on the cement and apparently ate a scrap of something. Purry was charged with interest. He stayed where he was and waited tensely until the strange cat turned away and went up the street. Then he crept hurriedly up to the same front door and smelled around it. He found a scrap of bread which tasted faintly of fish. It was stale, but he ate it hungrily. Then he found a few dry crumbs of fish. He searched until he was sure there was no more, and then slunk down the steps. He felt better. He had an urge to follow the other cat and see where it was going. But after sniffing and tracking it a little way, he decided not to stray too far from the place where he had found a bite to eat, and he began to poke around for some landmarks so that he would know this area again. He saw now that he must use his head. He had got lost from his home because he had not used his head, and now, while he hunted for it, he must learn to cope with this inferno that he had been flung into. There was at least one other cat coping with it. Now a new feeling stole into his blood and stiffened him so that he felt less likely to collapse. Suppose he was in the other cat's territory and would be attacked? He had to be on his guard. He couldn't spend his days and nights hiding.

So he began to be different. He moved in a different way like a cat taking stock of its situation. He prowled. He investigated the objects and spaces around him and calculated what he would do in case of certain happenings. He felt a kind of humming inside and a new interest in life.

Daylight came faintly with that peculiar cold that it always has. The air smelled fresh and clean. And now startlingly he began to see more cats. A little female as black as coal and bulging widely with a family that seemed about to be born appeared from under one of those monsters which was standing quietly by the side of the street. When standing still, those things could even furnish shelter for a cat, and many stood still all the time. The female did not see him, but went trotting away and paused in front of the house where he had found the scrap of bread. A gray-striped cat came and settled itself among some ivy in a flower box below a window. Finally the dirty gray one came across the street and sat in front of the same house. They all seemed to be waiting. There was something special about this house. None of these cats noticed Purry, since he was hidden in a bush in a cement pot.

He waited and dozed. When the sun was up and bright slices of light fell slanting along the street, the door of that house opened quietly, and an old woman, wearing a scarf around her head and pulling a faded purple bathrobe around her, peeped out furtively, stooped, and set a pan near the door. She made some whispering, hissing noises—it all seemed very secretive—and all three cats shot up the steps and began to gobble something from the pan. The woman withdrew and pulled the door shut softly.

This was his only chance; no matter how frightened he

was, he had to take it. He leaped up the steps and pushed in among them. The two males snarled. Purry bristled to defend himself and ward off a few swift swats of a paw. Another cat arrived, and there was growling, hitting, and spitting. Meanwhile Purry snatched a few bites. He did not get much, but it was enough to keep him going. After their hasty meal the cats dispersed rapidly, and while Purry was lingering to lick at a little gravy stuck on the side of the pan, the door burst open and a man charged out shouting and flourishing a newspaper at him. Purry plunged over the edge of the stoop into an open cellar window. There he found himself in a dim place full of pipes, tanks, piled-up boxes, and dust. He did not dare to explore. Above all, he could not risk being shut in. So he collected himself quietly on a ledge under the window. With a little food in him, he felt that this would be the right day for him to find his home.

He prowled, tramped, and hunted all day, but he did not find it.

# Chapter 15
# *The Underworld*

*So* Purry became a stray cat. He got used to his new condition slowly, and sometimes he felt that he had always been a stray cat. He even felt like a very old cat who had wandered the streets of an inhospitable creation from its beginning. There was nothing to hope for, nothing to expect. Life became a bleak process of scavenging for food, scrambling from destruction, defending himself against attack, hunting out a hole to sleep in. He was filthy with dust, soot, cobwebs, grit, and mud, and it was useless to clean himself. He was always thin and hungry and his eyes took on an expression of hard, indifferent, impersonal enmity toward everything. He still remembered that long, long ago he had lived in a house like these houses with their cold fronts and closed doors, and that there had been someone named Ann who loved him and set dishes of warm food in front of him, and a little cat named Bitsy whom he had cuddled and adored. He had even had a mother. But he did not believe all this any more. That was not the real way of life. The real way of life was to struggle against all other creatures for your existence, to creep, slink, hide, fight fear, be on guard every instant.

But in the midst of this harsh and dreary time he was finding out a great deal, and bit by bit he took an interest in things. He became acquainted with other stray cats in the neighborhood and learned how they lived. It was a kind of underworld. Stray cats were not supposed to exist at all. Nothing sanctioned them, nothing recognized them as a lawful class, and everything was always trying to get rid of them. Luckily for the cats, there were a few people, all old ladies, who sided with them, but it soon appeared that these people belonged to the underworld too and had to conduct their operations silently, usually under cover of dark. The old ladies, like the cats, were outlaws. They walked hurriedly, hunched over paper parcels, and looked back over their shoulders with a fugitive air. They would come to a regular place, usually late in the evening, where the cats had already been waiting for an hour or two. They would spread out the parcels hastily, sometimes pouring milk into paper cups, while making a hissing sound under their breath. Then they hurried away, leaving the cats to manage. Now and then there were fights and much noise. Then a window opened somewhere above, a voice shouted furiously, and a great splash of water fell.

Purry knew two of these places now. One was the house where he had got his first scrap of food; the other he found the next day by following the little pregnant female. He had to cross two streets to get there, and the streets threw him into fright, but he learned from her how other cats traveled. She ran the whole length of the block underneath the parked cars, and emerging at the end, she waited for a quiet moment, threw a rapid look all around, and made a quick dash across to a car parked opposite. Purry made it safely, keeping his eye on her. He saw her leap up on a curb and disappear around a corner. He followed intently, and between the bars of a big iron gate he caught a glimpse of her just vanishing back into a spacious area where there were garbage cans, a kind of shed, and several doors. He noticed that just inside the iron gate there were some paper plates and overturned paper cups with the smell of food about them. He decided to wait around. Before long the cats began to gather. The black female emerged from the shed door, a scrawny yellow one came in from the street; the same dirty gray one he had seen before, and finally a handsome little black fellow with a single white spot like a button on his breast. Purry remained hidden from the others and watched. They were all waiting, scrutinizing everyone who passed by. Some people paused to look at them, and the cats fixed their large, round, intense eyes upon each, trying with all their feline perception to determine whether that person would feed them, drive them away, or merely regard them with curiosity. They paid less attention to men, but every passing woman they watched with suspended hope. At last the right one came, hunched and hurrying, with a scarf around her head tied under her chin and a paper bag. They all recognized her as a species known to cats, a creature who shares the dangers of their existence and conspires with them to keep them alive. She snatched the used paper plates, shook some food out of her bag onto them, poured some milk into two paper cups, and hastened away. Purry crept out of his nook to join the other four, but they did not take to him kindly. They spat and struck, driving him back. You were supposed to have your settled place in these groups and be known to your fellows. They didn't want strangers. Food was too scarce. Purry didn't know how you were expected to establish yourself in such a set-up, but he was going to keep trying. This time he got only a few mouthfuls along with a few scratches in his face. But he would learn whatever strategy and pugnacity were needed.

The next morning long before sunrise he was waiting under a parked car on the street in front of his first feeding place. He managed to get a little breakfast there, and then took off in a great hurry to the place by the iron gate, where he arrived in time for a few more nibbles. So by calculating the time, by hurrying and waiting, by pushing his way in, and by fighting when necessary, he succeeded in getting enough food to keep him alive. But for every bite he got, he had to shoulder others away, even after they knew and unwillingly accepted him.

One day he saw the little black female come out of the shed where he had sometimes seen her go, and she wasn't bulging any more. Somewhere back there she had found a place to hide her family. She looked lank and shaggy now, and she was very hungry. She was fierce too. She would not let any other cat come near her shed. When

Purry tried to explore back there in search of a place to sleep, she came flying at him, bristling with claws. That was her corner, and the others had to respect it. Yet she had to go far afield in search of food. She visited all the feeding spots for blocks around with that lean, harried look of a mother who has young to support, and he often saw her hastening furtively across streets, keeping a sharp lookout for every danger, on her way back to her family. She never forgot that they were waiting trustfully for her return, and that if she should meet with any accident in the street, there would be no more milk for their eager mouths.

Purry never found a decent place to sleep. He forgot what real sleeping was like—those bygone drowsy afternoons when he could curl up on a pillow and slumber profoundly without a thought or a dream of danger, and the cold, rainy nights when he lay snug in the hollow of a blanket. Now he never fell into a deep sleep, but always kept his consciousness near the surface so that he would be jolted awake by any slight noise or movement near him. He tried many places—the shrubbery against a wall, corners underneath steps, a flower box by a porch, crannies anywhere among the numberless little spaces around buildings, especially those enclosed areas behind barred gates where in the daytime there was usually a man banging the garbage cans about or piling up castoff pieces of furniture. In the dead of night these places were quiet, and a cat could always get into them through the bars, though people could not. They were the only places where a stray cat could stay long, but there was never a comfortable spot anywhere in them—nothing but cold cement. In one of these areas Purry found himself a hollow where some bricks and cement had crumbled. He curled up on a rubble of brick, stone, and broken glass, with a drain pipe sticking out over him. It was not a good bed, but he was protected on three sides. During the day the sun shone in it briefly and he could catch a quick warm nap. But then one night it rained, a slow drizzle mixed with snow. He huddled back in his hole and listened to water dripping onto a piece of tin somewhere near. Soon it was dripping from the drainspout above. It made a little puddle which began to run back underneath him. So he came out into the cold, miserable dark to try to find himself another place. It rained all night. There was nowhere to stay except beneath a parked car. A cold wind blew around him, and a little stream of dirty water trickled by in the gutter. It was a long and dreary night.

Purry knew by instinct that winter was coming. All the cats knew it. The weather would turn bitter cold, the snow would pile high, the wind would come cutting across the large open space of the river. They needed to find themselves some kind of shelter, and each one was busy looking for himself. They all knew that houses have warm interiors, although most of them had never been inside a house. But it is easy to see even in one peek through a window that houses are comfortable inside, that they are dry and cozy with soft things to lie on. Tempting food smells come from open windows. But houses are hostile. The people in them know that if once they give you a bite to eat, if once they let you in, they will never get rid of you. And so, even though they have nothing against you personally, they keep driving you away. Most of the stray cats had little hope of finding a home, and if they had never had one, they were afraid of houses and people.

Purry knew several of these wild strays. One of them was the handsome black male with the button-like spot on his throat. He was a staunch and self-possessed little fellow who seemed quite equal to the risky world he lived in. Furthermore, he had made up his mind to find a real home of some sort, and he would sit watching, with an air of calculation, the doors that people went through and the windows where they appeared. How can a cat who has never been touched by a human move into somebody's house? But this was an unusual cat, and he did it, as Purry had occasion to learn later.

He had been born and grown up with three other young ones in the big woodsy park across the busiest street and down a hillside, and perhaps some old women, on their trips to feed the pigeons, took scraps to them. Then they learned to forage for themselves, to cross the crowded street between cars, to seek out the feeding places and keep safely out of the reach of every human while at the same time accepting most of their livelihood from human hands.

Purry and White Button came to be on friendly terms, a fact that gave relief to Purry, for he and all the other males were on fighting terms. Since he had not yet reached his full growth, he did not want to fight. He preferred to circle around his enemies and evade them rather than to come up face to face with some big fierce fellow who would challenge him about territory and female cats. Purry wasn't much concerned about female cats yet, and as for territory, he was forced to go on from wherever he found himself. Still, when necessary, he would stand and huff up his fur, utter horrible noises, and advance step by step in a bold attempt to make the other retreat. But White Button, like himself, was a young cat, and he was already a remarkable one. He would not fight except when forced to, and only in self-defense, but nobody bullied him. One day he and Purry sat looking at each other uncertainly. They both moved a few steps closer with the conventional hostility in their bodies. Purry began to make a warning sound in his throat. Then they sat still and looked at each other again with friendly eyes. At last they moved close together and each lifted a paw to ward off the other's attack. But they touched noses lengthily and each moved his nose over the other's face with great interest, still holding a paw in readiness. Then Purry wondered how they were to withdraw, since in the cat world you cannot back away with dignity, and if you turn, your opponent will likely attack from the rear. The first to withdraw admits defeat, and so two cats must sometimes sit for hours facing each other and making an occasional hideous noise when both would rather go home. But White Button declined to follow such a silly code. He had made his overture of friendship, and now he simply turned and went about his business. Purry followed. When he got to the end of the block, he saw White Button's shiny black rear hurrying across the wide street toward the side where there were no buildings. Purry did not dare to venture out on that busy highway.

But another time, late in the night, he followed White Button again to the same place. It was the still hour when night has come to grips with morning and they cling deadlocked for a while. This is the time when nearly all traffic and footsteps have stopped and when cats feel the hum of daring in their blood. Purry made it across the street and then slunk along a low wall under big trees until he saw his guide turn to some stone steps that went far down into a well of darkness. Down those steps Purry crept with all his senses alert, and at the bottom he found himself in what seemed a dense forest. It was frightening, for he was not a forest cat, he was a back-fence cat. As he padded over the ground, there were rustles and noises in the dank, dead leaves, sounding very loud in the stillness. The air was full of muggy mist, and now and then from far below came the long, soft moan of foghorns on the river like big gentle animals trying to communicate with each other.

Now he saw White Button moving stealthily through the bushes ahead as if he knew where he was going. Purry followed, and in a moment he saw a small cement building among the trees. The other cat leaped up to a narrow high window and disappeared. Purry snooped around this structure and found that there was no other opening, for the door was shut tightly, and so he too leaped up to the window and peered in. He could make out a mess of things on the floor—they seemed to be paint buckets, garden tools, rolled up hoses, crates, and some big plants with their roots wrapped in sacks. In one corner somebody had thrown an old coat, and on it were huddled several cats who began to snarl at him.

Purry would have liked to move into this shelter, but he knew he would not be admitted by the family of cats already in possession. He jumped down again and continued poking around outside, hoping to think of some diplomatic approach. But when faint daylight began to come, he withdrew and made his way back through the woods, up the steps, and across the street in order to be on hand in good time at his breakfast place.

Purry wanted desperately to find himself another home. It was useless to think of his old one. But he yearned so for a warm place, a soft cushion, a clean dish of food, a long sleep without fear. He began to try all the front windows that he could reach. But nobody seemed to understand how badly he wanted to be taken in. If he sat quietly and wistfully waiting for a window to open, nothing ever happened. But if he scratched and meowed, someone would come and shoo him away. Comfort and happiness belonged to a past dream. A stray cat has to make his way in the world as it really is.

## Chapter 16

# The Right Turning

Purry woke in the dark hours of morning from his cold, cramped sleep against a stone wall. A high wind was blowing. Everything rattled, banged, and flapped. A piece of glass crashed and shattered near him, and he bolted from his cranny, scampering up the walk amid gusts of leaves and tatters of paper. He fled across a street and sought refuge under a car, where he crouched listening to a garbage-can lid clanging down some steps. Then he ran on, dodging into any place that looked like a shelter. If only he could find somewhere a snug kitchen with a stove and a refrigerator in it, if only he could curl up safe for a few hours, he wouldn't mind so much having to live in the street with danger on all sides the rest of the time. Somewhere in this wilderness there must be an open window.

He scurried across another street or two, persistently

trying those closed fronts, and then, amazingly, he came upon two wide-open windows close to the ground, or rather he discovered, as he poked around, that there was no glass in them behind their curved iron bars. They opened into a big, black, vacant space full of wind. Evidently nobody lived there. The emptiness was frightening, but there might be some place inside where a cat could snatch a little sleep. He slipped through the bars, jumped down onto some boards, and made his way noiselessly all through the length of an abandoned building which seemed to have no insides at all. At the far end he found that the back too was open, and he emerged onto soft earth, finding himself near a board fence on which the wind was banging and flapping a loose slat. All this began to seem hazily familiar to him. He had almost forgotten board fences, but there was an affinity for them far back in his feelings. He leaped up and padded softly along it. It seemed so natural to be there.

He felt uneasily that he must not risk being lost from his feeding places. But something was drawing him now. His head stopped thinking. Something drew him along by itself through the flapping, swaying windiness. He padded on silently, and at a certain corner he turned by instinct and moved toward a house where there was a dark barred window open at the bottom. He climbed through that window as stealthily as a ghost and was greeted by a muffled cat sound. Two gleaming eyes watched him. That little cat was not a stranger. She came close and they nosed each other, making soft sounds of recognition. He crept around a kitchen floor and into another room. He seemed to know this place from long ago.

Now there was the sudden creaking noise of someone getting up from a bed. Purry shrank underneath a couch just as a light was turned on. Someone stooped, and he was staring into a surprised face that he knew.

"Purry!" Ann cried. But he was too frightened to move. Ann jumped up and ran to the kitchen, and then he heard the most heavenly of all sounds to a long-lost cat—the slam of a refrigerator door. A moment later he was eating liver and chicken while he rumbled with ecstatic purring, and Ann stroked him over and over, talking to him joyfully. He was home again, he was back in paradise after ages of inferno. He was back where he belonged, where someone wanted him. He had found his way home. And how utterly easy it was if you just came to that right turning.

Bitsy kept trying to get his attention, but he could not think of her yet. It was all too much. He remembered her very well, but he could not feel everything at once or include her in his first gladness. He did not see his mother, Bug, for she was out having her own little prowl at that hour. For the present he could only think that he was home again and that he was being fed and stroked. When he had eaten all he could, Ann went back to bed, and Purry, all filthy as he was from ten days and nights of living in holes, jumped up and lay close beside her, purring as hard as possible to express his profound contentment. Never did a cat have a deeper, a more blissful sleep. He awoke, purring again, when the sun was shining outside.

For several days Purry followed Ann around. He stayed near her all the time, lying by her feet or climbing onto her lap whenever he could. She brushed him and brushed him until he began to feel clean again, though it was a long time before his white breast and feet looked white. He washed himself tirelessly now that there was some point to it once more. How he loved to feel clean rugs and cushions under him!

He did not pay much attention to Bug and Bitsy for a while, a fact which was agreeable enough to Bug—she accepted him back with calm, but she did not want to be bothered by her big son any more. But little Bitsy had missed him very much. With no playmate, she could think of nothing to do. Sometimes she had simply sat in the middle of the floor and uttered a few forlorn meows about nothing in particular. Now she was full of happiness to have him back, and kept trying to coax him into a romp. She could not understand that he had been through a lifetime of experience during the ten days she had pined for him, and that he could not be lighthearted yet. It would take him a while to come back to his irresponsible playfulness with Bitsy, now that he knew the solemn facts of the world outside.

But little by little he returned to his old ways, and Bitsy was delighted when he raced with her around the house and garden and when he licked her face and neck as of yore and bullied her, though she still got angry and spat before it was over.

It was some days before Purry wanted to climb the fence again. He was satisfied not to stir outside his own yard; he knew now that everything a cat could want was there, and that this itself was the kind of spot homeless cats dream about. But after a time, when he had slept, rested, eaten, washed, and played with Bitsy until he felt normal again, he decided to take a walk and see his old haunts. So he strolled up and down the fence, and he even went to have a look at that empty building through which he had been tempted by the tantalizing daylight at its far end. The workmen were still pounding there, but now it was almost closed up. He could no longer see daylight through it. He was a lucky cat to have found his way home in time.

But he was a little sorry to see that this passage between the two sides of the world was closing. Not that he had much of an urge to try the boundless other side again. But he liked to know that he could if he wanted to. He liked to be reminded that it was there. He was glad that he knew about it. In its own way, it was a good world—you had to be awfully sharp there, and it is interesting to find out for yourself whether you can be sharp enough. His old acquaintance White Button got along very well and seemed to enjoy his life. Purry wished there was a way to move back and forth from that to this—if he could only be sure of being able to get back. For neither cats nor people want to be safe all the time.

# Chapter 17
# *A Ladylike Mishap*

*It* was indeed an unlucky autumn, for now Bitsy too vanished for a time into the realm of lost cats. And Bitsy was no adventuress. She was a shy and feminine little cat who never went far from home and never stayed long. Poor Ann was again roaming the neighborhood, peeking into entranceways under steps and through barred gates back into little alleys between walls. In Purry's case she had figured out very soon what had happened. But now the building that he had passed through into the street was closed up and finished, and besides, Bitsy was not a cat to go seeking new territories. She liked to stay in the places she knew. Ann also had an idea as to what had happened to Bitsy, but there was nothing she could do about it. She guessed that Bitsy had been coaxed in through somebody's window and the window closed behind her. And in fact, while Ann was poking in cellarways, Bitsy was lying on an expensive Persian rug yearning for her home.

It started over one bite that Bitsy tried to snatch from Purry's bowl at dinner because her own bowl contained some pieces of rubbery kidney, which she didn't like much, and she thought Purry might have something better. He never did, though she never felt sure of that. But her attempt was thwarted by Ann, who insisted on each cat eating from its own bowl. Bitsy was offended. She would have liked one mouthful of something nice.

Later when she was out taking her evening promenade, she saw through a window a young man lifting a large roasting pan from an oven. It contained a huge turkey that stuck up high out of the pan. The window was open at the top, and a strong, delicious smell drifted out on the cold air. Bitsy sniffed and wandered over where she could get a closer view. She found herself a good observation point on the fence just a few yards from the window, and she sat watching, wadded into a neat round ball. The man, who had a pale, blotched face and a small beard, came and opened the window from the bottom to let out more steam and aroma. He saw Bitsy and called to her. But she was always shy of strangers, so she sat still, looking very dainty. The man shouted to someone in the next room, and another young man came to look at her. They stood there at the window talking and gazing at Bitsy with interest, while she tilted her head to one side and looked away.

Now Bitsy was really a pretty little cat. When she sat up on her haunches with her small head delicately poised, she had a long, slender elegance. Her fur was fine and fluffy, especially on her throat, and although it was black all over, only its surface was black; underneath it was a soft cottonish white.

Now she drew herself up and turned her profile, and for a moment she looked like some expensive art object on display in a showcase. The two men looked at her and talked to each other as if they were considering buying something for a collection. Then one of them called her again and laid a sliver of turkey on the outside ledge. Bitsy decided to accept it, but she took her time getting over there, pretending to be quite used to such courtesy. It had a most savory taste. She accepted another piece which was laid on the inside ledge. She was frightened by a great deal of noise from the next room—the sound of voices, feet, and music—but the turkey was delicious, and she could see how huge it was. She had never seen anything edible as big as that, and something told her that she could have as much of it as she wanted. The next little sliver was put down on the edge of the sink, and then the window was quietly closed behind her. The two men were telling each other that winter was coming and perhaps she needed a home. She could live here, and they would keep her shut in for a while until she got used to them and the place. Of course Bitsy did not look in the least like a stray cat. Quite the contrary, she had a manner as if expecting certain refinements and even some pampering. Not that soft living was to be had at Ann's house. Some cats simply have a gift for looking that way.

But now more people came noisily into the kitchen, and she was startled by so many. She jumped up to the window, hoping to have more turkey served on the outside ledge, but now to her terror she found herself a captive. Someone snatched her up and carried her into the midst of a lively crowd. Bitsy made a frantic leap over somebody's back and scrambled under a couch, and there she stayed, as far back in the corner as she could get, for several hours. People stooped and peeped at her and called coaxingly, and after a while little scraps of turkey and other good things were pushed back to her. But she was too upset to eat any more. She listened fearfully all evening to the many noises: the scraping of numerous feet, loud music from a phonograph and a piano and then from a horn, the clatter of bottles and glasses, dishes and silverware, and later on, singing and shouting. She could not imagine how she would ever get out of here and get home. There seemed to be hundreds of feet shuffling around in her view, and as the evening wore on, some became wobbly and uncertain, while the voices above wavered, rising and drooping. Then there were a couple of loud quarrels and something crashed and shattered. Now the front door opened and shut frequently, the numbers of feet decreased, and things quieted down. Bitsy wondered whether she should try to make a dash through the door when it opened, but she could not make up her mind in time. Someone was trying to coax her out again, but she would not come. Finally the lights were turned off and people went to bed. Those who had fallen asleep around the room stayed where they were.

After a while when all was still, Bitsy crept out and tried the windows, but she found them all closed except a small one with a wire grating over it. She began to meow desperately. A man got up from bed and came to pet and comfort her. He carried her back to bed with him, but she would not stay there. She poked around most of the night scratching at windows and meowing.

Bitsy lived in that apartment for nearly two weeks, and she was very well treated. There were always many young men around, and everybody who came petted her. Lots of expensive steaks and other foods were brought in and offered to her. Plenty of soft pillows and rugs were at her disposal. She could sleep on anybody's bed. She got used to her captors, and they competed to get her on their laps. But every day and every night she cried plaintively to be let out and tried to find some opening. She was always trying the front door, but she was put back inside before the hall door opened.

At first the commotion of this life kept her nervous. She never knew how many of these men lived here, for so many were going in and out all the time. They cooked and ate incessantly and stacked the dirty pans and dishes in the sink. Then others would come in and explode in fury when they found they had to wash up all the dirty things before they could cook, and Bitsy would shrink underneath something until she saw that these explosions were no danger to her. Afterwards they painted pictures, played the piano, clacked the typewriter, and had loud discussions most of the night, and Bitsy found that she could climb around over their various occupations, disregarding any spurts of violence. Eventually some went away, but there were always a few left to sleep on the beds and couches.

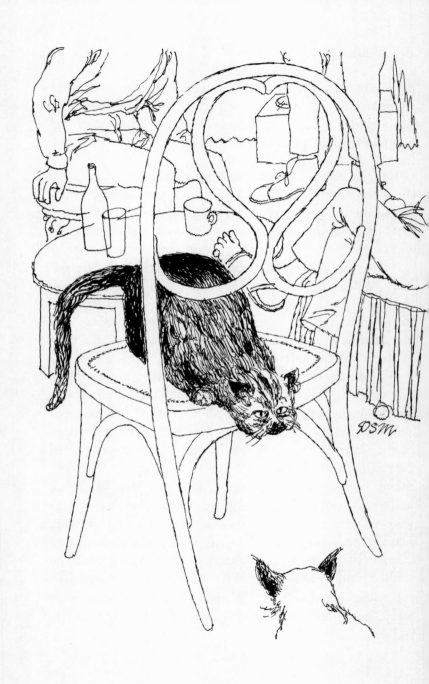

The one with the little beard who had first seen her from the window was more constant than the others, and he seemed to be her chief captor, for he took the most care not to let her escape. His name was Hanky. He had taken a great liking to Bitsy. He called her pet names, rubbed his face against her fluffy throat, and let her sit on the table beside his plate while he ate his dinner, feeding her the nicest tidbits. Bitsy like him well enough. He was a small, slender nervous man who was always having highpitched arguments with the others in an excitable shrill voice. But while he was screeching at someone, he was usually stroking Bitsy and trying to feed her a bite, so she learned to pay no attention to his fits. After his quarrels, he would sulk and refuse to speak, and at these times he wanted to hold Bitsy in his arms against his chest. He had a way of behaving as if without her he would find himself alone in the world. He needed her as his pillow against everything. Bitsy felt this need, and she didn't object to her role. She liked to be coddled. But then she innocently hurt his feelings by climbing on another person's lap or choosing a different bed to sleep on.

There was so much here that she had to get used to— so much furniture, so many knickknacks, so many clothes and shoes, so many glasses and bottles, so many mealtimes, and so much scuffling around. Every day some new piece of furniture or ornament or contraption would come into the house, and after Bitsy had nosed around it and tried to get used to it, there would be a big dispute and it would go out again. Records for the phonograph were always arriving and being tried out at a volume that scared Bitsy under the couches. New china plates or figurines were set on a shelf, and once Bitsy had the bad luck to knock one off and break it. But no one thought of her, and there was a big quarrel. Once several of them decided to paint the alcove where the dishes and bottles were kept, and Bitsy spent a day crouching under things to keep out of the confusion of paint pails, ladders, and displaced glass.

But this indoor life was not enough for her. She wanted also to cope with outdoor problems to keep her muscles and claws in trim and to be in command of cat strategy. She grew thin. Steaks, turkey, and salmon palled on her, and there did not seem much point in eating when there was no Purry to compete with. Why should you gobble down your food if no other cat is trying to snatch your share? You may as well leave it to eat later, and then later you forget about it. She would no longer even come when they called her from the kitchen. They had conferences about what they should buy for her, and they kept trying different things. Now she would often turn away from a dish after barely tasting it to see what menu they had thought up for her. Hanky coaxed and pleaded. It grieved him to see her refuse food— although he often did the same thing himself, and he too was thin.

Far from becoming reconciled to her life, Bitsy sat in the window and meowed more plaintively than ever, gazing out and yearning for a breath of cold air. Now the late November rains fell mixed with snow, and strong winds shook branches and shrubs. But she wanted to be out.

The inevitable happened one night. Hanky came home with a basket and took from it a beautiful Siamese cat with black legs and a golden body, and he set this expensive-looking creature down face to face with Bitsy. The two stared at each other and their backs went up. They retreated under different beds and from time to time expressed themselves with growls and ominous little wails.

Late that night at bedtime when Bitsy was sitting on her kitchen window sill uttering an occasional complaining sound and Hanky had finally coaxed the Siamese cat out from under something and onto his bed, he came to the kitchen and quietly opened the window. Before Bitsy realized what had happened, she was out on the ledge; then she was on the fence running as fast as she could and meowing at the top of her voice.

Ann was sitting at home under the reading lamp when she heard a lot of meowing in the distance coming rapidly closer, and she knew who it was. She had waited days and days for this and had somehow known that one night Bitsy would come running home like that from wherever she had been kept all that time. A moment later Bitsy came leaping onto the couch, over Ann's lap, and around the room. She could not stop running. Ann followed her around crying, "Bitsy, Bitsy!" But it was a while before Bitsy could calm down. She had to smell everything before she could be sure that she was at home. Then she ran outside to the yard and all around it, sniffing everything, while Ann followed, until she came to a special post of the fence which the cats always sharpened their claws on. She reached up, stretching herself out full length, and scratched and scratched for five minutes at the usual place. That made her perfectly happy. She felt good scratching at the old post like that. Now she knew she was at home, and she quieted down. She let Ann pet her, she touched noses with Purry and Bug, she suddenly felt hungry and wanted to eat, for she had grown quite thin. And how good a rubbery old piece of kidney tasted! The food here was nothing much to speak of—it was quite ordinary, but they always ate it like pigs and wished for more. Then she slept peacefully all night. When all is said, cats simply want to be at home where they belong.

In after days she sometimes strolled past that house where she had been held captive. Once in a while she saw Hanky with his blotched face and little beard, but perhaps he was very near-sighted, for he never seemed to see her, or at least to look as though he had ever seen her before. The window was always closed, and often the beautiful golden Siamese cat sat there, fastidiously washing its black paws and gazing out with disdain upon any passing common-cat traffic. But anyone could see that it would have liked to come out and discover what went on along board fences. Still, such a beautiful cat can never roam around safely. It is better not to be too beautiful if you can possibly help it, when even an ordinary little cat like Bitsy is sometimes kidnapped.

# Chapter *18*

# *A Very Remarkable Cat*

*I*t is time to tell the story of White Button and how he came to live at Ann's house. For weeks he had been making every effort to find himself a home for the winter, but his problem was an almost insuperable one: he would never let himself be touched by any human being. He had nothing against human beings. Some were kind to cats, some were unkind, and most were indifferent. But since he had grown up wild, his nature told him that it was not safe to let any of those creatures touch you.

Still, he had many qualifications for a house cat. He was a handsome young fellow, all jet black except for the white spot on his throat. Gifted with poise and dignity, he always seemed ready for some formal occasion, and he gave the impression that he would know how to conduct himself in any company—a curious talent for a cat who has never been inside a house. Besides, he was a pacifist.

He accomplished the feat of finding a shelter and some security without fighting and without displacing anybody. Not that he was seeking a safe life for himself. A stray cat understands in his bones that there is no such thing as safety, that every day is a dangerous day by natural law. He loved all the challenges. But he wanted a warm place where he could go to evade the worst weather and where he could count on a little food.

So he systematically canvassed his neighborhood, and in due course he invaded the block where Ann lived. He found his way up the stone wall at the end, as Bug's old lover and a few other cats had come and gone, hazardous the first time, but all right when you knew the footholds. He came over the top, through the small trees and bushes, and onto the board fence, along which he walked for a short distance taking a look around. Then he withdrew and made sure of his way back down the wall. That was his method. He took everything slowly and planned his strategy. The next day he came again and had a longer look. He walked along past several yards and sized them up. In one there was a yapping little dog that made a lot of noise at him. That one was out of the question. In the next house he heard a clamoring parrot, and he decided to pass that one too. A parrot might be hard to win over. In another house he saw two children in a window, so that one was out.

In a few days he grew familiar with this block, and there was one place that specially attracted his interest. He counted three other cats who all seemed to live there, and they created a problem, for nobody knew better than he how hostile cats are to an invader. A stranger is an enemy. On the other hand, a place where so many cats lived was bound to be a good place for cats. These all seemed well off, and the person who sometimes appeared in the window looked as if she would be all right. Furthermore, one window had a little square opening at the bottom, just big enough for a cat to go through, which was always there, day and night. The three who lived here could go in and out whenever they pleased. White Button liked this arrangement. Before long he observed what time they usually had their dinner in the evening, and once while they were all busy eating, he came quite close, stretched his neck, and got a good look from the fence near the wall. He could see all of them, and amazingly they were all eating from separate bowls. In fact, each cat had two bowls—a yellow one for food and a red one for milk. There was no fighting or spitting as at the places where he ate. White Button liked this procedure. He felt it would suit him, since he had nice manners by nature. He would like an orderly life.

Soon after this Ann noticed that her cats were developing an odd habit. When they had finished their dinner, they would each get up on something around the kitchen —one on top of the cupboard, one on the refrigerator, and one on a shelf—and sit there looking through the window. They seemed to be expecting something to happen. One night they all became alert at once. Ann looked out, but she could see nothing, for it was dark now by six o'clock. Then she perceived two shining eyes and a round white spot under them, which remained stationary for a while, then moved off and disappeared. It seemed there was a mysterious evening caller who uttered no sound and did not wish to make his presence known.

The next night Ann turned on an outside light, and she saw that their caller was quite a handsome fellow who sat drawn up in a huddle. He was well-behaved, and the others felt no menace in his presence. Apparently he wanted nothing, and he soon went away. Ann supposed that he belonged to some proper household.

White Button continued to pay these visits every evening, and nobody objected. One night when Ann saw him in the light getting settled in his usual place to watch, she noticed that he was much thinner than she had known and that he had a wistful look in his eyes. Now it dawned on her that he was hungry. She went outside to offer him a scrap of meat, but he ran away from her. She left the scrap of meat on the fence, and he came back and ate it eagerly. After that, since he never made any noise or trouble, she took a little food out to him every evening. When she approached, he always ran off a little distance, but she left the dish, and then he came back to eat. So he became a regular boarder. Ann gradually realized that he was wild and shy and had never belonged to anyone.

After a while he began coming in the afternoon to lie in the yard and wait for dinnertime. The yard was cold and bare, not a comfortable place to rest in, but White Button did not mind. He had no better place, and it was peaceful here. No one bothered him. Since he was perfectly quiet, Bug, Purry, and Bitsy grew used to him, and they would all go out to look him over. He never made any motion against them, and they accepted him as a kind of funny new species of harmless creature. He and Purry had a vague memory of having been formerly acquainted, and they touched noses carefully. But since Purry was the male of the household, he felt now and then that he ought to question this fellow's right to be here, and several times he tried giving White Button a bat with his paw. White Button answered calmly with exactly the amount of repulse that was necessary, and the two batted each other smartly for a moment. But it was only an exercise to establish mutual respect. Again they touched noses, each with one paw half raised, but White Button never struck first.

Still his problem was not solved. The weather was growing very cold, so cold that he sometimes woke stiff, as if he had congealed during his sleep. He knew it was warm in the house, but he was afraid to go through that opening in the window. Ann called to him and invited him in, but he did not trust that sort of thing. This Ann was very nice, and he was glad to know her, but what would she be like if you were shut up with her in a house? These other cats thought she was perfectly safe, but then they liked sitting on laps and being petted. White Button had no intention of ever getting that close to a human. A stray cat knows that he can depend only on himself, and that he can take care of himself only as long as he can see a clear way out of everything. An unknown place with one small opening is a place he cannot afford to investigate, even though three other cats live there safely enough.

So how was he to manage, now that had found the house he wanted? He continued to sleep curled up in the bare yard, and when the wind was too cutting, he would go to seek out one or another of the holes he knew.

One afternoon at dusk it began to snow, the wind turned bitter cold, and before long the air was thick with streaks of sleety snow driving slantwise. This was White Button's first blizzard; the winter before he had been a kitten hidden in some protected corner and nursed by a warm mother. Now he had to learn to cope with blizzards. He visited all his dinner places and got enough to eat, and then he made his way down into the park to the little cement building which he still shared with two or three other cats. This was the only place he knew where he could weather a blizzard, and it was not going to be very good. The old lady who came down that way to feed the pigeons and leave a few scraps for the cats could not come so far in such weather as this. The wind blew in through the small, high window and swirled around, and the old coat that somebody had left in a corner for them to lie on was already crusted over with sifting snow. As he curled up there with the others trying to sleep, he thought of the warm place where Bitsy, Purry, and Bug lived and of the little square opening in the window. About midnight he made up his mind to go and have a look at it.

All the way up through the park he went, scampering over the deepening drifts with the stinging wind and snow against him, across the icy street and along the familiar block of houses, down the stairway, over the concrete area, up the jagged wall, along the fence to Ann's yard. Little drifts fell off on both sides of the fence as he plowed his way. Once there, he sat near the win-

dow and uttered a few plaintive sounds. All was dark, but he could see the little black opening with its curtain over it. After a while he saw Ann's face appear dimly in the window. She lifted the little curtain and called to him softly. She wanted him to come in from the storm. But White Button was afraid. He sat there for a while trying to think of something, but what could he do? To a stray cat whatever is known, no matter how bad it is, is safer than the unknown. So after a while he went off into the fierce night and made his way back to his cold shelter in the park.

But he did not give up trying to solve his predicament. He knew that the winter would last a long time. There had to be a way for a cat of his ingenuity to become an occupant of that inviting warm place.

The snow remained on the ground many days. Then it softened into a slush, and rain fell, and the streets were deep in slop. Then came a freeze and all was ice. Meanwhile, like any stray cat, White Button went about his business and got to all his feeding places in time. By now he had observed a useful fact. If he came back to Ann's yard after making his dinner rounds, he noticed that often she was not to be seen. She evidently went away through a different door and did not come back for several hours. While she was gone, he might dare to enter that house. Since humans cannot move without a little noise, he would be sure to hear her coming back in time to make his exit.

One evening when Ann came home late, she saw a black tail disappearing quickly under the small curtain. Bug, Purry, and Bitsy were all lying around in their usual places. She turned on the outside light and saw White Button's rear vanishing over the fence. After that, every time she came home late she witnessed this same scene. Then she found that there was a warm spot on the couch where he had been lying. The others were perfectly peaceful. They felt no uneasiness about him, for there was not a hint of aggression in his manner. He only slipped in quietly and rested for a while on the couch until he heard footsteps outside the front door. When he was gone, the others sometimes sniffed curiously at the spot where he had been. But nobody minded having him there.

This strategy worked very well, but it did not settle White Button's problem. It was only a way of snatching a bit of comfort once every two or three evenings. Ann hoped that he would get used to her and not run out into the cold when she came home. But with his tact, manners, and good looks, he was bound to improve his condition.

Soon White Button made another useful observation. He could see that after the lights were turned off at night, all was quiet inside. Ann was there, but she was not moving around. If he crept in, making a soft little sound so that the other cats would know who he was, he might snatch a nap. He discovered that she stayed all night on one side of the room, and the couch that he liked was on the opposite side. If he heard her stirring around, he had time enough to leap up and be gone. Bug usually slept on the foot of Ann's bed, Bitsy had a box back in the closet, and Purry slept around in different places. It disturbed nobody if White Button stayed qui-

etly in the spot he liked all night and was up and out at
daybreak. Before long he was spending most of his nights
there instead of in the cold little park building. He felt
very contented about this. Slowly his problem was working itself out.

But now he thought how nice it would be if he could
come in the daytime too. So Ann helped him work out a
scheme. She folded an old piece of blanket and put it on
the chest which was under the cats' entrance. Then she
shut the kitchen door and stayed in the other room, and
White Button came creeping through the window and
rested on this little bed for a while. He scrambled as soon
as the door opened. But from that stage it was only a
matter of time until he gradually got used to everything.
Now the door would be left open, and Ann learned how
to come into the kitchen without frightening him. She
sidled past, not coming near, and he lay there warily
watching her every move as she cooked and washed
dishes, ready to jump if she came a step too close. Bitsy,
Bug, and Purry stepped over him as they went in and
out. They considered him as harmless as a piece of furniture. He and Ann formed an understanding: on his side
that he would be perfectly clean and quiet and make no
trouble at all; on her side that she would not come too
close and would never try to touch him.

All this took a long time, but slowly through the winter
White Button established himself. Gradually he came to
feel safe when he curled up on the couch, and free to
come and go when he wished, though it was not really
until the next year that he would sleep like a kitten all
day while Ann walked around him within touching dis-

tance. At last he was a cat with a home, but he was as free as ever to roam the streets, to eat at his old places if he wished, to live any kind of life that he wanted at any moment. Now and then he disapppeared for a day or two, and then suddenly at dinnertime he showed up at the window, gently pushed his way under the curtain, and seated himself, looking up confidently at Ann with his soft eyes. She never touched him, but sometimes he came near and touched her ankle with his paw while she was getting their meal ready as if to ask, "Did you count me?"

And how he loved to sleep snugly on cold nights in his favorite spot while the wind or sleet or rain drove against the windows, and to know he was welcome here. He was perfectly happy. He felt that there could be no better life for any creature.

White Button was a good cat to have around, for he became a kind of peacemaker in the neighborhood. Once in a while Purry or Bug had squabbles with their semi-enemies, and if White Button saw a skirmish shaping up, he would come moseying along and let his presence be known. Bug still had a feeling of resentment against the old white cat. In reality he was a mild fellow who had nothing against her. He had been in the vicinity long before she was born and didn't care much what went on, but since she was always expecting some rudeness from him, he sometimes obliged by waylaying her on the fence and just sitting there like a road block until she went into a rage of frustration. Then White Button, if he was handy, jumped up behind the white cat and merely sat there yawning and washing his paws, just in case he might be needed, and before long it all broke up without incident. Or in the middle of the night when there were angry catcalls far down the fence, White Button softly got up from his place on the couch and went out the window. Nobody knew how he managed, but soon the noise would stop or retreat into the distance. Then he stayed out the rest of the night to keep an eye on things and patrol his district. He considered it his job to maintain order in that area.

He kept his independence. He belonged to nobody but himself. He made his own decisions and assumed all the responsibility for his life. He kept in touch with his old places and acquaintances, since, having grown up as a stray cat, he would never be so flippant as to give up a good thing altogether. He knew that anything might happen. The kind people might disappear or change their minds and want to get rid of him, and so he never relied wholly on anyone.

White Button had seen large, fat, sleepy cats blinking from windows, cats who had the illusion that life was soft. But he knew how things really were. He liked the danger, the cars whizzing by, the crowds of people never to be trusted, the new encounters, the excitement of every new day. It would be difficult to say what cats were created for, but perhaps they were only created to enjoy their lives. Anyway, White Button enjoyed his, and he was a very superior cat.

# Chapter 19

# *A Very Special Cat*

Anyone who was around Bug for a while would soon see that there was something very special about her. Nothing obvious, nothing to be noticed at once. At first glance she seemed just a routine black-and-white house cat. She would have to be called a "common" cat by whoever does the classifying. But nothing about Bug, from her inmost self out, was quite common. In the core of her being she was highly refined, sensitive, mysterious, and intense, and her inmost nature showed in a subdued way all over her. It showed most in her eyes. She had a deeply serious look in her eyes, sometimes a troubled look as if she were trying to understand the strange and intriguing outside world from somewhere far inside her.

There was something spiritlike about her whole being. Compared to her son Purry, who stomped around with a masculine air, his head up, looking very bold, Bug had a delicacy and lightness of figure, a neat round contour, and fur of a special live, soft, glittery texture. She had a way of moving along with liquid, slithering curves, hardly touching anything, always with that look of secret wonder as though she had just seen or expected to see something that no one else would believe. In shadow, the black pools of her eyes opened full and round. When she came out into bright light, they closed to narrow vertical slits until nothing but gooseberry-green iris was left, as if she drew curtains over her secret abode and became just any sleepy cat in the sun.

She no longer had any attachments in the cat world. All that business of lovers, husband, kittens, and domesticity was finished and behind her. She had been through it with her whole heart and the best of cat passions. But now she wanted to be free of all that, not to be tied down any more by love and worry and by creatures who needed her, but to be let alone to draw within herself and live her hidden life.

Of course she could not escape the ordinary world. She had to cope with it, especially those two young ruffians, Purry and Bitsy. In her heart she felt a stable affection for them and was satisfied to have them around. But she was glad that they had each other to romp and quarrel with. Their silly habit of licking each other's faces lovingly and then beginning to spit and bite was revolting to Bug. When she was so annoyed that she could not keep her feelings under cover, she would give one or the other a swat with her paw. This provoked reprisals, and sometimes she got mauled, a treatment that she hated above everything. It threw her into a frenzy. But more often,

Purry thought her tempers were not worth that much trouble, and instead of pouncing on her, he would merely stare at her offensively until she felt indignant and insulted. She had long forgotten that he was her son and thought of him as a lummox who took up too much room. He was too big, too clumsy, too affectionate, too stupid. He was a nuisance that she had to put up with around the house and avoid when she couldn't endure him. But plainly he thought himself important, and he liked attention. He purred louder than any six other cats together, and he was always purring as if every moment he expected to be petted and made a big fuss over. Ann was very fond of him, and that too annoyed Bug. She couldn't see anything so wonderful about that fellow.

Purry took it for granted that he was good-looking, and he liked to be well groomed. Once Bug sat opposite him on Ann's writing table and watched him for at least ten minutes washing and washing himself as if preparing for some special occasion. She regarded him with loathing as he sat there licking noisily, and suddenly, unable to suppress her disgust any longer, she reached across the table and smacked him. Purry set down the paw he was washing himself with and stared at her. Then with a snort he continued. Being smacked by this fastidious cat who used to be his mother was hardly worth much notice.

Bug thought that neither of those two was very sharp-witted, and she couldn't resist making fools of them. One of her tricks was to walk indifferently across the room as if she were going to pass by Bitsy and go out, and then, just as she passed, whirling around to give Bitsy a swift bat with her paw. Bitsy was always taken by surprise, even though at another time she might shy away from Bug and circle around her. Bug was too acute for them. She found their amusements naive. Sometimes against her will she was drawn into one of their games and found herself getting excited. But then there would be big Purry hiding behind a door, his rear end wiggling with eagerness, waiting to jump out on her, when all the time she could see him plainly through the crack on the hinge side. When he finally peeped around to see what was keeping her, she swatted his face. But she really preferred to ignore both of them. They were such a crude young pair.

Still, Bug was very playful herself in a subtle and agile way and with great imagination. But she chose to have her games in solitude or with Ann, who understood her tastes. The game most thrilling to her was called "ghost." Ann's part was to cast some spot of light on the wall from a shiny tin lid or mirror, and Bug would go chasing it in a frenzy of delight. Fairly mad with rapture, she bounded up over furniture and bookshelves after that elusive wisp of light. She rolled on her back with all her feet waving, her eyes wild, as if she were having a vision of something other-worldly. Yet she knew she could never catch that wisp of light, for when she had her paws on it, she could not see it at all but would look around crazily everywhere. It seemed to represent all the wonders that were beyond her grasp. But she never tired of trying to grasp them. Ann only needed to say, "Ghost!" and she began to look wildly around the ceiling. Neither Purry nor Bitsy could ever see any ghost at all, though Purry, when he

was half grown and still trying to do everything his
mother did, would jump up on a shelf and look around
agitatedly, pretending he saw a ghost. But there was not
even one to be seen when he did it. Later he gave up
trying to imitate her. She was too spiritual for him. Her
feelings were too high strung. He was just a normal boy
cat.

Another of her games was a very kittenish one, but this
too became especially mystical for her. She imagined
that her tail was a separate creature. She waved the tip
of it stealthily and peeped around, watching from the
corner of her eye, then suddenly whirled and pounced,
spinning and spinning until she fell and rolled on her
back in ecstatic dizziness. Her tail, like the ghost, could
never be caught, and it was the unattainable that en-
tranced her. She always played these games where Ann
could watch. Then with sudden and ineffable lightness
she would leap into a paper bag and hide.

The only being that Bug was attached to now was Ann.
Not in an obvious way, but in her own secretive, silent
way, not letting anybody else notice, and she felt very
secure about it. It didn't arouse her jealousy to see big,
chummy Purry jump up and flop on Ann's lap ahead of
her and sit there purring like an engine. She could wait.
She didn't have to compete with that sort of thing. Her
own procedure was a very delicate one. She would hover
around first to be sure that Ann was settled for a while
and that there was room for her.

She was interested in everything that Ann did. She
liked to spring up on the kitchen sink and crouch there to
watch with concentration the vegetables being peeled or

things being stirred in bowls. From the shelf above she had a good view of the dishwashing, which she could hardly take her eyes from. But most of all she enjoyed puttering among the papers on the desk. She touched them gently, curling her paws inwards as if trying to pick them up and figure out what they were. Then she would contrive to shift some of them aside and insert herself artfully between the papers and Ann's attention. This maneuver was always successful, since both found it amusing. They had the same tastes and they understood each other. They loved the quiet days when nothing particular happened, especially a rainy November afternoon when they could curl up together on a couch in the dusk and between naps gaze out the window at the drizzle beating on a dull, soggy garden. It was like withdrawing to some source where everything came into being out of stillness, and they soaked up their mutual solitude as the ground soaked up the rain. This was the focus and root of Bug's life now that her loves and passions among her own kind were over.

But she and Ann had their separate lives too. Ann went out the front door, and Bug the back, and neither knew what became of the other during those hours of absence. When Bug saw Ann getting ready to go out, she would sit quietly and watch her with large, absorbing eyes, trying to estimate from what clothes she put on, especially the shoes, how long she would be away. Not that any of them minded being left alone, but still Bug felt wistful when Ann closed the door and was gone. She wanted to know when to expect her back. She was curious as to what lay beyond the front door, and she took every opportunity to slip into the hallway and peer out. But she had no intention of ever going any farther.

Ann was just as curious about the back. She could not imagine all the things there were for cats to do out there, and she wondered how Bug busied herself for so many hours at a time or why she came in with that never-exhausted look of wonder in her eyes. What does a lady cat find, when her love days are over, to keep her so engrossed in life? Normally she would always be caught in the closely packed cycle of maternity and never have to think about what to do next, for everything would come of itself. The whole process would happen to her over and over without her choice. But here was Bug, her life still ahead of her, no longer bound to that treadmill. She could look at male cats more objectively, regarding them as friends or enemies instead of inevitable fathers of families. And there was always something going on that she had to cope with. New situations arose, due to the constant changes in the cat personnel of the neighborhood. It never failed that when she had a working relationship of some kind with every cat around, so that she knew when to run, to fight, or just to sit and hold her ground, some shift would upset the balance. An old-timer would vanish and a newcomer would appear from somewhere, wanting to establish itself, so that all the crosscurrents of feeling were disturbed and had to be readjusted. Bug took the role of the senior member of her family and one of the most legitimate inhabitants of the area, having been properly born in a proper home and well brought up. So it was up to her to know what was going on. Bitsy usually lost her head in an emergency, and Purry, though dependable, was a little slow. But now she had White Button to help, and they worked together. He was a wise fellow, and he always knew what he was doing.

In the spring a new troublemaker invaded, and White Button, pacifist though he was, turned warrior and took it upon himself to get rid of this prowler. It took him three days to do so, and during all that time he scarcely had a meal. He slunk by along the fence, wild and furtive, his whole being caught into that underworld of danger and daring where cats must often live outside of houses while all the coziness and soft pillows inside them are forgotten. He came to the window a few times, looking scrawny and driven, to lap thirstily from the squirrels' water dish, and took barely a minute to eat a bite of the food that Ann offered him before he was off, back to his post at some strategic passage point. The battle was still to come. So far there had been a few skirmishes and a lot of stealthy maneuvering.

Most of this time Bug too was out and could be seen now and then slipping hurriedly along the fence, her body low, with a most intent look on her face, engrossed to her core in this wily warfare which she understood so well. Then one night there were fierce and horrifying yowls from somewhere, rising to wails, and then a great commotion of scrambling, snarls, and shrieks swept all the length of the block like a cyclone, seeming to drag half the block with it. A little later Bug came in with her fur bushy and glittering, her tail fluffed out like a great plume. Her eyes reflected the light and glowed green and blue. She was like a beautiful wild animal of the forests.

The next morning White Button came peacefully to breakfast with a long scratch above his eye. The war was over.

Now that they had earned their serenity again, and spring and summer had come again, Bug spent the long middle of her days sleeping in the yard curled up among the violet leaves, and the ailanthus trees sprinkled a shower of tiny green blossoms over her, making her fur fragrant. The two squirrels twitched around in the branches, and Bug awoke to watch them with sharp, suspicious eyes. They whisked jerkily down the trunk together with scratchy noises and came to see what had been left for them, in the way of nuts or seeds on the window sill. One squirrel was pregnant, and she waddled as she ran. But that didn't keep her from getting around as fast as necessary, and she was always out of reach when Bug sprang and gave them both a lively minute. After streaking up a tree, they circled around and came back down to finish eating their peanuts. They knew very well that she would spring again and that they would be out of her reach in time once more. Meanwhile Purry awoke from his nap in the canvas chair and eyed them sleepily, and Bitsy came yawning out of her box in the closet to see what was doing. They figured that squirrels should be chased now and then to be kept alert and in trim, just as cats must prowl and fight to earn their peace. Such is the natural way of things, and they all understood it.

*A Note about the Author*

*Augusta Walker* was born and grew up in Cincinnati and
was graduated from the University of Michigan, where
she won an Avery Hopwood Prize for Fiction. She spent
three years teaching in China during the Communist
take-over, and her first novel, *Around a Rusty God*, grew
out of that experience. She has since had two other novels
published; several of her stories have appeared in *Yale
Review*, *Partisan Review* (which awarded her a fellowship),
and *Antioch Review*. She now makes her home in New
York's West Eighties, the setting of this story.

*A Note on the Type*

This book is set on the linotype in Caslon, so called after William Caslon (1692-1766), the first of a famous English family of type-designers and founders. In style Caslon was a reversion to earlier type styles. Its characteristics are remarkable regularity and symmetry, as well as beauty in the shape and proportion of the letters; its general effect is clear and open, but not weak or delicate. For uniformity, clearness, and readability it has perhaps never been surpassed. In 1843 Caslon type was revived by the then firm of Caslon for William Pickering and has since been one of the most widely used of all type designs in English and American printing.

This book was composed and bound by The Haddon Craftsmen, Inc., Scranton, Pa., and printed by Halliday Lithograph Corp., West Hanover, Mass.